CW01395179

ALIVE & KI

Twelve Australian legends share their secrets
of energy and vitality.

Carol O'Halloran

© Carol O'Halloran 2006
All rights reserved
No part of this publication may be reproduced or transmitted, in any
form or by any means, without the permission of the author.

First published 2006 by
Fitness Company International
Phone: (02) 9311 3235
PO Box 304 Matraville NSW 2046 Australia
Email: info@feelyounger.com.au
Web:www.feelyounger.com.au

National Library of Australia
Cataloguing-in-Publication data
O'Halloran, Carol.
Alive and Kicking!
The secrets of energy and vitality as told by Australian legends
ISBN 0-646-45561-3
1. Health,
2. Vitality
3. Exercise
4. Aging-Prevention
I. Title.
613

Edited by Tim Marlowe
Demarlowe Seminars and Consulting
tmarlowe@ozemail.com.au

Cover designed by
Sean Turner of Villani's Graphic Design
www.villanis.com.au

Typeset by
QL Graphics
www.qlgraphics.com.au

Book Print & Project Management by
Food For My Brain International
www.FoodForMyBrain.com

"I enjoyed Alive and Kicking so much. It makes me want to get up and conquer the world with energy!"

Mandy Worth – age 16

"I think everyone over 30 should read this book! It's inspiring and motivational and makes me feel like I'll have to go out there and do something with my life! When you're under 30 you think you're invincible, but after that you realize you're not!"

Nicky Cossar – age 36

"I found Alive and Kicking to be delightful - and even at my age I found it very helpful!"

Brian O'Halloran – age 91

"Carol has captured a considerable amount of information on the day-to-day habits of these 'famous' people. This makes the book a 'good read' and provides a quite unique opportunity to gaze through the window of their lives

Professor Morris, University of Sydney

CAROL O'HALLORAN is a well-known health and fitness speaker and TV presenter in Australia, South–East Asia and New Zealand. Carol has produced four videos, a gold best-selling exercise record and trained hundreds of fitness instructors on techniques for older and overweight clientele. She is the author of Five Minute Fitness and her home weight-loss program, Slender Secrets, screened on television throughout Australia and New Zealand.

This book is dedicated to my Dad, who at the age of 91 is bright, 'with it', flexible, fully independent, open-minded, still driving and loves to shop! An inspiration to all who meet him.

This book is a fascinating collection of personal accounts of lifestyle, habits and views of a selection of very well-known older Australians. Carol O'Halloran has captured a considerable amount of information on the day-to-day habits of these "famous" people. While the beautifully written stories on each are entirely anecdotal, there is an attempt to glean a few key messages about what makes these people tick. The opening lists some of the current concepts on healthy living, many of which were enunciated at a "Life Extension Symposium" held in Sydney. These are not connected with the rest of the book, but it is interesting to see how many of the principles enunciated have been adopted by the diversity of characters in each chapter. Not surprisingly, the people interviewed for the book partake of ways of life that are in accord with the particular generation they belong to. These people are definitely not health fanatics. They are extraordinary people who live very busy lives and it is informative to see what measures they take to cope. Many of their decisions and principles of daily living are certainly healthy, but this is to be expected for a collection such as this who are clearly intelligent and cognisant of the preferred choices for life enhancement and quality of life into the later years. The habits of each vary markedly, as one might expect for any group of people like this. Their philosophies about the inevitable end of life we all must face should provide inspiration to many who read this book. Each has an uncanny ability at articulation of deeply personal thoughts. This makes the book a "good read" and provides a quite unique opportunity to gaze through the window of their lives. Carol O'Halloran is to be congratulated on putting this all together in an eminently readable and enjoyable manner.

Brian J. Morris, PhD DSc FAHA
Professor, School of Medical Sciences
The University of Sydney
Sydney Australia

Table of Contents

ALIVE AND KICKING!

Chapter 1

The Dance is Forever and the Dance is You

How do YOU dance through life? Do you dance at all? Have you forgotten how to dance? At what age do you think you're going to stop dancing? Will you ever stop? How do we keep dancing through life to 90 and beyond? Is 90 old? Do we ever get old?

Ageing and getting older means different things to different people. My interviews with dozens of people showed that middle-aged could be perceived as anything from 35 to 100, and old age somewhere between 60 and 120! Life expectancy could be anything between 60 and 103, with the majority expecting to live to 90. Only two people saw themselves as being old, one was 88 and the other only 34! (What does that say about how they view life?!)

For the vast majority, 'old' is someone who is 10 to 15 years older than themselves, so most of us never get old! Many regarded 'old age' as something related to ability or mobility rather than age. As soon as you became frail and not able to function independently, you then became 'old'.

Ageing is a universal phenomenon in nature and the good news is that by making some simple decisions, you can take your foot off the gas pedal and slow down your rate of ageing. How you age is largely controlled by you. Follow the tips and learn the secrets from those in this book and you may never become 'old'.

You can't help getting older, but you don't have to get old
Within a few decades the United Nations statistics on population ageing predicts there will be over two million people over the age of 100. I am going to be one of them, are you?

What images of ageing do you hold in your head and what quality of life do you really want to have as you get older? Chances are you're going to have to make some mental and physical changes to maximise your life on this planet. But the good news is that it is never too early or too late to slow down the process of ageing.

It's most likely that you will live to 80 or 90 years of age. Already there are 200,000 people over 100 in the world and the average life span for a Japanese woman is already 89. The Health, Labour and Welfare Ministry also reports that one in every 20 Japanese females has a high probability of celebrating her 100th birthday. The Australian Bureau of Statistics predicts that in Australia there will be 852,100 people over the age of 80 by 2016! The longest well-documented life-span was Madame Jeanne Calment who died in 1997 at 122! She took up fencing at 85 and was still riding a bicycle at 100! The good news is that if you reach 100, chances are you will remain independent and fully functioning up to the age of 92. (88% of centenarian females and 100% of centenarian males are functioning independently at that age.) The sad news, however is that women still far outnumber men in the older age group. There are 81 men aged 60 or over for every 100 women, and among the over 80 group, there are 53 men for every 100 women.

In Abkhasia, Russia the word 'old' does not exist and value in society is placed on longevity, hence a large number of the population survive to 100 and beyond. The later years are regarded as the most rewarding phase of life and growing old is a time for improvement. Sedentary retirement is unknown with workers continuing to do physical labour (reduced hours) at 80, 90 and even 100.

As George Burns said, 'You can't help getting older, but you don't have to get old.' There are many things we can do to slow down what we now view as normal ageing. So the question is – 'Are you going to sit idly by and watch your body deteriorate? Or are you going to take action to 'live to the max?'

It is the lifestyle choices you make which determine both how long you live and the quality of life you have.

You age, as does every living creature. It is part of the cosmic plan. But how you age is not, nor is your life span. I have interviewed dozens of people and many seem to think that they will be lucky to live as long as their parents, that somehow genetics determines their fate. It does not.

Inherited genetics account for 10-30% of all ageing effects. By the age of 80, behavioural choices account almost entirely for a person's overall health and longevity. Children do however inherit behaviours (eating & exercising habits) from their parents and these can affect the rate at which you age. No centenarian has ever been recorded as having had a mother or father who was a centenarian!

It is the lifestyle choices you make which determine both how long you live and the quality of life you have. And you won't just live longer, you'll live younger.

What is your age? Chronological, biological or psychological? Your chronological age you can't change, but by looking after your lifestyle habits, nutrition, exercise, relaxation, you can reduce your biological age 10, 20 or even 30 years. You can keep psychologically youthful by continuing to be interested, to read, to learn, to be open.

Stop thinking about health as the prevention of disease and start thinking about it as the prevention of ageing. Health is like money. Health decisions and behavioural choices that you make today are capital toward living younger tomorrow.

According to William Evans and Brian Rosenberg, these biomarkers of age can all be reversed through exercise and diet:

1. Lean Body Mass – the amount of muscle you have. Muscle mass affects your metabolism, your strength, and gives support to the skeletal system.

2. Strength – the loss of strength that occurs with age can be lessened through exercise. Strong quadriceps, for instance, have been shown to reduce the likelihood of falls, as you get older.

3. Basal Metabolic Rate – exercise and thus muscle mass

both elevate your basic metabolic rate, that is the amount of calories you burn even at rest.

4. Body Fat – affected by both nutrition and exercise. Excess body fat is linked to obesity, diabetes, high cholesterol, arteriosclerosis and high blood pressure. Men and women carrying an extra 30kg are 3000% more likely to develop diabetes. Even being moderately overweight increases your risk of diabetes by about 100% and also increases your chances of prostate cancer, colon cancer, and breast cancer as shown in a study by the American Cancer Society.

According to Arthur V Everitt from the Centre for Education and Research on Ageing, in Sydney, a sedentary life style in Australia has led to overeating which is life shortening. Our intake of calories should be reduced from early life. When the food intake of rats or mice is restricted by 40% from childhood, many physiological ageing processes are retarded, the onset of most diseases is delayed and the duration of life is extended by about 40%.

Similar studies have also been done on monkeys, and the inhabitants of Okinawa in Japan are living proof that calorie restriction appears to have an impact on longevity. Okinawans consume 40% fewer calories than Americans, are smaller in body size, and have much lower levels of heart disease and cancer. In 1996 there were 34 Okinawan centenarians per 100,000 of population, the highest in the world, compared with 10 in the USA.

In Australia 67.7% of Men and 52.5% of women are classified as being overweight (National Cardiovascular Disease Database 1999-2000).

5. Aerobic Capacity – by age 65 the body's ability to use oxygen efficiently has declined 30-40% and affects our ability to be fully functioning on a daily basis. This can be increased by exercise.

6. Blood Pressure – can be reduced with exercise, salt reduction and nutrition. Blood pressure is the amount of force exerted by blood on the walls of the arteries as it flows through them. The higher your blood pressure, the

more stress and strain you are putting on your body. High blood pressure is linked to the possibility of stroke and heart attack.

89% of Americans have blood pressure higher than the ideal for preventing aging. 1.5 million Americans suffer heart attacks every year and half a million have strokes, approximately one third die as a result. 40% of all women die from arterial and coronary problems, ten times the number of women who die from breast cancer. In Australia 35% of males and 42% of females die from circulatory diseases (Australian Institute of Health & Welfare 2000).

7. Blood Sugar Tolerance. The ability to use glucose in the bloodstream declines with age, raising the risk of Type 2 diabetes. This can be improved through dietary changes and weight control. Approximately 7% of Australian men and women are diabetic (1999-2000 Australian Diabetes, Obesity & Lifestyle Study).

8. Cholesterol/HDL ratio. An elevated cholesterol reading increases the heart attack risk. Both nutrition and exercise can lower cholesterol. Taking folate regularly may also help keep lipids (fats) from building up in your arteries.

9. Bone Density. As we age our bones tend to become more brittle. Weight-bearing exercise and nutrition will both improve bone density.

10. Body Temperature Regulation. Older people become more vulnerable to hot and cold weather. Body temperature can be regulated through exercise.

According to the Harvard Medical School Report on Cancer Prevention 1997, approximately 50% of all cancers can be prevented by a better diet, exercise, decreased alcohol use, smoking cessation and using common sense with the sun. In Australia 30% of males and 25% of females die from cancer (Australian Institute of Health & Welfare 2000).

90% of lung cancers and one third of all cancers diagnosed in Europe and the USA can be linked to tobacco use. Every cigarette you smoke is a choice you make to get older faster.

Within 12 hours of quitting your body begins to get younger. Your blood can carry more oxygen to the cells in the body and in only a few weeks damaged nerve endings in the mouth and throat begin to regenerate and the bronchial tubes begin to open.

Effective Stress Management Techniques

Learning how to manage stress is also an important lifestyle skill. According to psychiatrist, Dr Maja Stanojevic-Andre, stress today, and especially psychosocial stress has reached epidemic proportions with up to 70 to 80% of doctors' visits stress-related. She suggests that meditation is a very worthwhile strategy. "Meditation is one of the most powerful tools for prevention and management of stress reaction, and whatever is going to decrease stress reactions in the body is going to prevent aging and extend life".

Studies by Keith Wallace, a physiologist at the University of California, showed that those who had been meditating longer than 5 years had an average biological age 12 years younger than their chronological age.

Don't Forget Your Largest Organ – Your Skin

Everyone needs some sun every day. Sun allows our bodies to produce Vitamin D, which is an important nutrient that helps decrease aging of the cardiovascular and immune systems. 10 to 20 minutes of sunlight a day appears to be optimal. Your risk of skin cancer is determined by how much sun exposure you received in your youth. People who had severe sunburns as children are at much higher risk of skin cancers than those who never burned.

Ultraviolet C rays cause the highest rates of cancers. Australia and New Zealand are at particular risk because the ozone layer is damaged permitting these damaging UV C rays to enter. Regardless of age, you can take steps to minimise further sun damage and wrinkles!

One thing is guaranteed: You will get older each and every

day, but it is you who are responsible for your successful old age. 'Many of the aspects of being old that were considered due to the intrinsic ageing process are really related to lifestyle.' – Dr John W Rowe, McArthur Foundation Research Network on Successful Aging.

When you take care of your body, time slows down. You will have more time – time to be what you want to be, and to do what you want to do.

Every single one of us can do things to start getting younger. You make the choice about how you want to age or not. Your skin replaces itself every month, your stomach lining every five days, your liver every six weeks and your skeleton every three months. By the end of a year, 98% of the atoms in your body will have been exchanged for new ones. The physical and mental lifestyle choices you make today decide how you will age in the future. It's not just longevity we're after, but the vitality, energy and quality of later years.

Strategy for age reduction

The Director General of the World Health Organisation said in 1999: "In our ever-changing world the ageing process is one of the few things that unifies and defines us all. We all are ageing, and this something to be celebrated. Whether we are 25 or 65, 10 or 110, ageing is a life-long process of change. While ageing is commonly associated with specific age groups, for example those 60 years and older, ageing as a process continues throughout the entire life-span. However, the way we age and whether we maintain a high level of health and activity at older ages are largely determined by individual actions."

The objective is to not only live longer but to live healthier. You can slow the rate at which your body ages. The payoff is not 30 years away, but now. Why get old when you can stay young?

We know we need to drink more water, eat less processed foods, animal fat and sugar and eat more fresh fruit and vegetables, fish etc, but is this enough? The nutritional value of these foods has become severely depleted. For example, according to the USA handbook for Recommended Dietary Allowances, vitamin C 'may be considerably lower because of destruction by heat and oxygen', peas lose 83% of their vitamins by serving time, and we would have to eat 75 bowls of spinach today to get the same iron content as one bowl 50 years ago.

We often hear about the recommended daily allowance or RDA, but this is the minimum needed to prevent disease from deficiency. We should start thinking about the recommended optimal amount, or the dose you need to stay as young as you could be. A study by Dr Chandra on 96 healthy elderly men and women found that vitamin takers had only half the number of days of debilitating infectious illness as those on the dummy pill.

The Antioxidant Advantage

Antioxidants can help prevent the oxidation damage that has been linked to cancers and other types of ageing. As we know, oxygen is necessary for our body to function. However, while oxygen is needed for our cells to function, it also forms oxygen radicals or free radicals (now termed 'reactive oxygen species' or ROS) which oxidise or damage our tissues, much as when you see a car rusts, or an apple turn brown after you cut it.

These oxygen free radicals are an unstable form of oxygen which can cause genetic damage, leading to cancer, premature aging of tissue and immune system damage. Oxidation also ages your arteries and makes them more likely to become clogged with fat deposits.

Antioxidants bind to these free radicals and prevent them from causing damage. An important antioxidant is Vitamin C, which can enter the centre of the cell and collect the free radicals. It helps to keep the arteries clear by inhibiting the oxidation of fat in the walls of your blood vessels. Another example is Vitamin E, which has been shown to lower the risk of heart attack in women by as much as 40%. Vitamin E works on the lipids that clog the arteries and thin the blood, making clots less likely to form. Very much better than these are antioxidants found in certain herbal preparations such as gingko biloba, green tea, etc.

According to a California Health Department study, if medical science could wipe out just one major health risk, arteriosclerosis (hardening of the arteries), the average life expectancy for women in California would rise to 100!

Antioxidants boost immunity and studies show that they can inhibit, prevent or even cure hundreds of diseases in addition to cancer, heart disease and diabetes. Antioxidants not only neutralise free radicals but also increase your resistance to toxins, bacteria, viruses, traumas, and degenerative diseases.

There is a plethora of information on antioxidants, and I recommend you speak with a nutritionist, naturopath or read 'The New Nutrition' by Dr Michael Colgan. They will all be able to help you evaluate a good antioxidant combination which will help strengthen your immune system and slow down the ageing process.

'Even older people who consume pretty good diets experience enhanced immunity by taking a multivitamin supplement '- Dr John D Bogden, (University of Medicine and Dentistry, New Jersey).

Maintain your sexual health

The Baltimore Longitudinal Study of Ageing on 800 men and women showed that remaining sexually active throughout one's early and middle years gives one the best chance of remaining active into old age. Married men between 60 and 80 had sex between 3 and 52 times per year. Most subjects believed that regular sexual activity was good for their health.

Another study done at Duke University, USA found that people who had more sex more often lived longer, and a study in Great Britain suggested that men who have sex more than the once a week average – that is, over two orgasms a week, have lower rates of mortality.

Accept the new and welcome the unknown

People don't grow old. When they stop growing they become old. It's important to be always learning and being willing to learn, new skills, new knowledge, new experiences and new ways of looking at the world. As soon as you stop 'being interested' in new things, in what's going on in life, you deteriorate. How often do you catch yourself saying 'I've always been like that, that's just the way I am,' instead of, 'The person I am today is different from the person I was last week. I love to learn new things; I'm open to new ideas and new experiences. I embrace the unknown because it allows me to see new aspects of myself. Change is exciting and helps me grow as a person.'

So many people seem to have given up on life in the 20s, 30s, or 40s. They have become narrow-minded, set in their ways and lack energy. Tao Te Ching said 'Whatever is flexible and flowing will tend to grow, whatever is rigid and blocked will wither and die.'

What image of ageing will you keep before you? Are you open to change? Do you accept the new, welcome the unknown?

What about age discrimination– does it exist? Unfortunately, yes. Several people interviewed in this book commented that with all their years of experience and knowledge, they felt younger people didn't value what they had to say and what they could contribute. In some workplaces people are hesitant to hire someone 50 or older. But this is changing; some companies now are more likely to hire an older person because they are more stable, likely to stay with the company longer, and have more experience to draw on.

It is sad that some people who have been made redundant in later years just seem to give up on life, the attitude being; 'Oh, nobody will give me a job at my age!' Again, this is a self-fulfiling prophecy. In your 50s you're only just over half way there, and with the growing ageing population there is now talk of putting the retirement age up to 70. If you believe you have energy, you will. If you believe you'll get a job, you will. Look at Colonel Sanders, who didn't start KFC (Kentucky Fried Chicken) until he had retired in his 60s!

It's mind over matter, or rather mind over 'being old'
Deepak Chopra says that he might see two heart patients afflicted with angina pectoris. One patient will be able to run, swim, and perhaps even mountain-climb, totally ignoring his pain or not even having any, while the other nearly faints with pain when he gets up out of his armchair. Every patient stamps his condition with a unique perspective; there is no single response for all people, it is very largely related to the mind/body connection.

In my own life I have seen people give up, take on negative destructive behaviours, and shut themselves off from the rest of the world. Others are out there, overlooking the aches and pains, trying things, always busy with friends and embracing life.

A dear friend of mine Lilly, at 75, like those interviewed in this book, is vivacious, lively, always looking forward to trying new things, new food, going to new places and meeting new people. She wears bright clothes and loves to dance, belly-dancing and flamenco. In other words, she embraces life in all its forms. Do you?

You are only as old as you think you are
The decline of energy and vitality in old age is largely the result of people expecting it to decline. It becomes a sort of self-fulfiling prophecy. The talk in people's heads goes; 'I am getting older, so I expect my eyesight to go. I should be slowing down. I can't do that any more at my age'. The despair of growing old makes you grow old faster.

I support Deepak Chopra's idea. He says that by repeating affirmations we can take control of our thought processes. By saying things to ourselves, like,' 'I want to improve in energy and vigour every day', or 'Today I wish to experience more youthful enthusiasm', you can begin to assert control over those brain centres that determine how much energy will be expressed.

Deepak also describes two levels of awareness – time-bound and timeless. Time-bound awareness is associated with ageing, confusion, fatigue, repression, and feelings of victimisation, conflict, sorrow, fear, anxiety and imprisonment in ego. Timeless awareness is associated with freedom, autonomy, youthfulness, unbounded energy, liberated emotions, peace, power, harmony and joy. You can consciously program your mind to remain youthful using the power of intention.

How often have you heard the saying, 'You are only as old as you think you are!' And how often have you heard, 'I'm too old to change!'

You can alter ageing by breaking out of old patterns–mental, physical and lifestyle patterns, and by changing your self-talk; "I am not older, I am better!!!"

The most meaningful thing you can live for is to reach your full potential.

Apart from positive self-talk, what do the inspirational older people you are about to read about have in common? They have relinquished the need for external approval. They know who they are, and are happy with themselves. They have let go of negative emotions such as fear, anger, sorrow, regret, greed, distrust. They have a purpose in life.

All the people interviewed in the rest of this book have a purpose, a challenge, an interest, a passion, something they want to do or contribute. It gives them energy. It gives focus. It takes the emphasis off the self and onto others. It gives them a reason to place their health as a number one priority. It takes them forward into their 90s and beyond. If you haven't already, I hope that you too will find your purpose, your passion, by the end of the book. Enjoy their stories.

Chapter 2

Jeremy Bingham

Jeremy Bingham was Lord Mayor of Sydney from 1989 to 1991, and prior to that was an alderman of Sydney City Council for 12 years and of Hunters Hill Council for 6 years. He was the Original Chairman of the Sydney Olympic Bid Committee, and as a result was an official guest at the opening ceremony of the Sydney 2000 Olympics. Jeremy was also Chairman of the Central Sydney Planning Committee responsible for all major planning decisions for the City of Sydney.

Jeremy was born in 1936, holds the degrees of Bachelor of Arts and Bachelor of Laws from Sydney University, and has been a partner of the national law firm Deacons (and its predecessors) since 1959. He is recognised as a leading expert in development, environmental and local government law and is a senior advocate in the Land and Environment Court of New South Wales. Jeremy has been a board member of the State Chamber of Commerce (NSW) since 1991, including two years as President.

Jeremy is married to Candy Tymson and has five adult children and five grandsons by two previous marriages. In 1980 he starting doing aerobics and became a gym junkie. Then at the age of 55 Jeremy started doing triathlons and he currently competes in the 65+ age group.

Just for something different Jeremy, at the age of 67, took up Theatre Sports, Mime and learning to Salsa. His triathlete mates call him 'Top Dog' – who said an old dog can't learn new tricks!!

It's better than the alternative!
There are compensations to getting older. The stuff that

used to drive me nuts doesn't matter any more. I think you become better at relationships, and I think you get more joy out of relationships. That's how it's been for me. The best thing you can say about the aging process is that it's better than the alternative – and the alternative to getting older is to be dead. Although I'm not afraid of being dead, it's the process of how you get to be dead which sometimes worries you a bit. You don't want to get Alzheimer's, or cancer, or whatever.

The expression 'middle-aged' and the expression 'elderly' both carry connotations. When people talk about middle-age, it usually conjures up for you the image of a bloke, someone who's got a gut, someone who's dull and boring. An elderly person conjures up for me someone who is frail and has difficulty walking. I don't like either expression, and I don't think either applies to me.

I once met a couple who were elderly. I identified them as sort of my parent's generation, a generation ahead of me. To my astonishment, I learnt that they were both younger than me. To me they were a whole generation older than me – their attitude, the way they looked, dressed, acted, spoke. I think the message is about looking after yourself, looking after your body and your mind, no matter how old you are.

Organise your work and personal life

Most of the time, I've got tons of energy; I bounce out of bed in the morning. I'm both a morning, and an evening person. I have no trouble waking up and starting the day, and no trouble working in the evening. I get 7-8 hours sleep and my energy levels are very high, my activity levels are very high.

I get up at half past six. I like to get up at the same time every day, except for Sundays. I think it makes life easier. I have a shower, get breakfast, have a look at the paper, hop in the car, and drive into town. I'm in town in the office usually about half past eight. Recently I've changed my pattern, I used to work every night until 8, often 10 or 11. This was 6-7 days a week. Now I'm trying to taper off a bit and not work past 6.30 at night, but sometimes it's still as late as 7.30.

I've had the habit all my life of working very long hours, and when I was Lord Mayor it was really a crushing pace. I used to work from 8 am to midday in the legal office, then midday to midnight in the Town Hall, and then midnight to 8 am I had time to get home, have a sleep and do the jobs at home. That was six days a week – Sundays we generally had off. It was a genuine 18 hour day doing two jobs.

My staff had to fit me into three one-hour, high impact aerobic sessions a week. Everything was booked in, so on Tuesday I'd have a meeting, then a conference with someone, then an official visit from an ambassador, and then one hour plus travel for my aerobic session. Then I'd get back for another conference or interview, or cocktail party, or speech or whatever. It was quite a standing joke at the Town Hall. I said "I don't care exactly when you do it, but you've got to get me to three one hour aerobic sessions a week". I'd also go on Saturday as well, so that made four times a week.

Always focus on the positive

I always focus on the positive. My attitude to every situation is, 'So that's not good, what are we going to do about it?'. So many people whinge, whinge, whinge, and tell me what 'they' oughta do. I used to call it the great Australian heart disease, AORTA – they oughta do this, and they oughta do that and they oughta do the other thing. Never mind what 'they', whoever 'they' are, ought to do, what are we going to do? What are you going to do? How are we going to do to manage this? What's our role in this?

This approach gives you a sense of control to some extent over what's happening and you're not just a victim. The opposite of enthusiasm and drive is being a victim; 'It all happens to me', 'O poor me', that feeling of helplessness and powerlessness that a lot of people seem to have.

I annoy them all in the office, because in the morning I

bounce in and I meet someone in the lift and I say 'G'day, Bill, how're you going? Isn't it a lovely day?' The response is usually something like 'Oh.. Not bad' and I say, 'Gee, what's wrong? How come, it's not terrific today?' and they all duck away from me. A lot of people spend their lives like that, where every day there's a whinge about something. It's whinge, whinge, whinge.

I sometimes go off about something which is bothering me, but most of the time I don't bother with things that aren't any good. I'm interested in what's good, what we can do, how we can improve it. Enthusiasm and a positive focus are the answer.

Negative emotions are not something to dwell on, and you should try to organise them out of your life to the extent that you can. You can't always do that – something terrible can happen and you can be overwhelmed with grief, or you can be thoroughly enraged. Do to the best that you can, organise your life, and seek the support of family and friends, who are loving, good fun, and good company.

Excuses don't get it done!

My wife Candy and I are founding members of the Brown Dogs triathlon group. We just attracted like souls, and triathlon has become a very big part of our life. The triathlon group is a great way to achieve a number of things which are very important.

In order to be fit, it's very hard to maintain a good exercise regime on your own. Most people get stuck at that point, even though they have good intentions. 'I'm going to ride my bike, I'm going to go swimming, I'm going to go three mornings a week, I'm going to go the gym'. If you try to do it on your own, human nature being what it is, there are always too many reasons why you can't.

One major piece of advice is that you've got to get friends. You've got to get a group, even one other person will do. You say 'lets meet at North Sydney pool on Tuesday evening at 6.30', and then you've got to be there. I believe when you've got friends to whom you're committed, you've got added impetus.

Everyone has the voice in the head which gives them all the reasons why they can't. The voice goes:'Oh I can't, I've got this work to do, I can't get there tonight, I haven't got the time, it's too hard and when I look outside it's cold and its windy or it's hot and its raining, or it's not raining, and I'm tired, and it's not fair, why should I have to do it'.

The voice goes yammer, yammer, yammer. If you listen to that voice, you won't do it. If you don't do it, you won't get the benefits of doing it. You can't stop the voice. The voice still goes on. Candy and I still have that voice yabbering away, and we've been doing triathlons for 12 years. Universally when I start a race, that voice is telling me NO, telling me why I can't, why I shouldn't, and why I should cop out. It's just there, don't listen to it! You can't turn it off, just ignore it.

When you say you're going to be there, Thursday, at the time and place nominated – be there. Don't say why you're not there, don't give an excuse. That's the big thing about life too. A lot of people think that there is no difference between doing what you said you'd do, and having a good excuse why you didn't do it. There's all the difference in the world. You either do it, or you don't do it! Excuses don't get it done, and I'm a great believer in doing what you'll say you'll do.

At the end of a race or at the end of a training session I feel totally different, an immense feeling of wellbeing. It's that endorphin feeling you get after a hard training session or a race. There just is nothing else like it in the world, it's the best feeling. You feel pleased with yourself and it doesn't matter where you came. I'm sure the endorphin feeling is the same if you come first or last, or anywhere else in the middle.

Just do it. Don't listen to the voice, make a commitment, and get friends to back you up.

On Saturdays, we get up at about half past six, load up the bikes and gear into the car and head off to Centennial Park to join the Brown Dogs Triathlon group. There we do a one-hour bike ride, and then scoot off to Clovelly Beach. Then we do a run along the cliff towards Bondi followed by a swim at Clovelly. We sometimes do a variation, like run/swim repetitions. This is where you run around Clovelly in your runners and costume, then dive in and swim across the bay, then run around again, dive in and swim across again. Five circuits takes about an hour, and at the end you're well and truly pooped – it's a great workout.

Tuesday night it's swim squad, which is serious swimming with a bit of a run beforehand, if you've got the time. On Thursday night it's a long run, with a bit of a swim afterwards. Sundays, Candy and I usually do something – a mountain bike ride, kayaking or go for a run locally. That makes four training sessions a week. We do it all year round, regardless of the weather.

Breakfast is very important
I'm a bit different from most people; I eat three times a day, I never skip a meal, I pay a lot of attention to breakfast and I don't eat anything in between.

With my medication I have orange juice with Vit C and a piece of fruit, which could be mango, peach or something like that. I have Yakult, with the bacteria for your gut. I take my memory assist pills, multi vitamins, vitamin E and shark cartilage for the arthritis in my fingers. I eat Sports Plus cereal with lite milk and sometimes I'll have a cup of coffee, but no fat. Lunch is something light, three times a week sandwiches in the office, salad, or chicken and salad.

I've been taking supplements and anti-oxidants for 13 years. I believe anti-oxidants are important; I've read about free radicals, and I believe it's worth doing. I took zinc for a long time because I was concerned I might have had prostate cancer, which fortunately I haven't. Now I'm just taking it as part of a multi-vitamin. When you read the information about supplements, it costs relatively little, and the potential benefits make it worthwhile.

Meals at home have always been fresh food, fresh vegetables, lot of salads and a lot of fruit. I'm also a great eater of potatoes. As I like protein, I mainly eat fish and chicken, and I consciously eat meat about twice a week.

I have a couple of little weaknesses, like just about everyone else in the world. I quite like French fries. When we eat out with my friends, the "Brown Dogs" on Tuesdays and Thursday night, I'm quite capable of having a steak or chicken, with salad and French fries. However, I must say we never cook French fries at home; in fact, we never cook anything in fat at home. We have Chinese takeaways occasionally, even eat pizza about once a month. My weight hasn't changed – I've been 75 kg now for 12 years.

When I was younger, I could have paid more attention to my diet. I don't think I would ever have smoked (I smoked for 20 years), and I wouldn't have drunk as much.

Do the best to improve the odds in your favour

My approach to life is that you do the best to improve the odds in your favour, but you don't know what's going to happen to you. Accidents happen, trauma happens, disease happens. You should do your best to improve your chances, eat sensibly, exercise sensibly, and sleep sensibly. Organise your personal life so that it's a good happy life.

Looking after your skin is also important. I rub moisturiser on my skin every day, and put block-out on my skin whenever I go out in the sun. I take Immodeen, which is supposed to put moisture into the skin, and I cover up. I wouldn't dream of going out in the sun without block-out on my face and ears, and a t-shirt and cap.

There is nothing to fear in getting older; getting older can have lots of benefits, but it's not something you would seek to accelerate. You should stay as young as you can, in terms of looking after yourself physically, mentally and emotionally, all three. People who self-destruct – physically, emotionally or mentally – either quit, or refuse to acknowledge that what they are doing is heading them down the path to disaster

– like smoking for example.

You're going to have to die some day, and you,re going to have to die some way. All you can do is say, 'I can't control it'. You can't control what is going to happen to you, but you can improve the odds. You can live sensibly, and do the right thing. After that, what's going to happen is going to happen, and thank goodness we don't know. If you become fit and enthusiastic, and have the right approach, you're going to have a lot better life than most people who are a lot younger than you!

Get on with it!

There are a few things about the aging process that aren't so good. Things break down and you've got to get them fixed, or you can't do things for a while, like shake hands without hurting because your fingers are so sore. But you get over that, and get on with it.

I had a minor stroke a couple of years ago. We didn't know why, because all my veins and arteries were clear as a bell. All the conventional checks couldn't find anything, and a whole battery of tests couldn't figure it out. They then took a look inside the heart and found I had a hole in the heart.

I had suffered for some time from arrhythmia, atrial fibrillation. They figured that some little speck of something that should have stopped in the lung got into the wrong chamber of my heart and pumped straight into my brain, giving me the stroke. They patched the hole in the heart with a catheter going up the femoral artery, without opening my chest up – amazing. I'm now on medication to prevent my heart from fibrillating, also blood thinner to make sure clots don't form inside my heart, and a beta blocker to slow my pulse rate down.

As an outcome of this episode I got a lot of anxiety. Apparently it's very common, but no one quite knows why. It's very, very disconcerting stuff, because I'd wake up at three in the morning and I'd be anxious. If you asked, 'What are you anxious about?' Well, the answer is you're anxious about whatever you're thinking about. It's a state, it's not a rational process; I'd be anxious about the roof, I'd be anxious about the car, I'd be anxious about my foot, I'd be anxious about anything.

I did a good session with an NLP practitioner and that helped me, and from there I had a huge amount of support from my wife Candy. I had a lot of difficulty with it initially. It took me nearly two years to get to a point where I reckon it's pretty well over now. Exercise has a hell of a lot to do with coping with states like that. The endorphins that you get. The feeling of contentment and well-being that you get after exercise is a huge antidote.

A few months ago I had my first colonoscopy, and they removed a number of polyps. They told me to go back in six months for a follow-up – even though they weren't cancerous, you can't help but be a little bit concerned.

Apart from arrhythmia, I used to get a totally different condition called tachycardia, which used to happen to me generally in triathlons. I'd come out of the swim, run into transition and my pulse rate would be about 120. Then as I put my shoes on and got on the bike it would jump to 240. At that rate you're not pumping any blood, your heart's going bang, bang, bang, bang. You can't do anything. I'd have to stop and wait and try all sorts of tricks to jump it back into rhythm.

The moment my heart stopped doing it, usually after 5 to 15 minutes, I'd jump on the bike and continue the race, but it always kept my times slow. But I'd never worry about it. As far as the arrhythmia is concerned it's totally different – your heart doesn't beat regularly, it skips a beat, and I just ignored it. But that wasn't the smart thing to do -I didn't appreciate that it could form clots in the heart.

I had been denying my mortality. I used to say, and I was only half kidding; 'If you're improving your triathlon times you're getting younger, not older.' Once this happened, I stopped trying to improve my triathlon times.

I've had to accept that I have reached that point where the thing now is to do a triathlon in good time, and trying to beat your personal best is not suitable. It's now a case of doing it to the best of my ability, as fast as I can, without becoming distressed.

Nobody cares except you!

Exercise is about doing it; it's not about beating other people, or even beating your own personal best. Lots and lots of blokes I know won't compete or do triathlons because they think they can't win, they can't beat other people. That's a stupid attitude; the whole point is doing it and getting the satisfaction of doing it, being pleased with how you went. It's perfectly possible to be pleased – I had a good swim, I had a good bike ride, I didn't get injured, to get through it injury-free, to get through it without your heart blowing up. That's a satisfying thing in itself. And the fact that a lot of people can do it faster than you has nothing to do with anything. It's not about proving that you're faster than other people. It's about doing it.... and that great feeling afterwards.

In my age group, if I enter and complete the course, I've got a fair chance of getting a trophy anyway, because there's often not more than three in my age group.

Be kind to yourself. Understand that doing it at all is infinitely better than not doing it. Don't set unreasonable targets or unreasonable goals. You shouldn't say for example; 'I should be able to run 10km at 5 min kilometres, that's 50 min for 10 km.' You shouldn't insist that you can do it that quickly. You should say – 'I'll do it in whatever time it takes.' Don't start with 10km. Start with 3km.

Lots of people, in fact it's almost endemic amongst men, think of what they used to do when they were younger. In their minds they say, 'Unless I can still do that, I'm not going to do it', so they don't do it. It's really just a cop out. The interesting thing is that when it's a question of how long does it takes you to run 10km or how long it takes you to do the triathlon, nobody cares except you! The rest of the world couldn't care less. Nobody cares where you come, nobody cares how fast you went, nobody notices. The only person who cares is you.

You're not in it to win. It doesn't matter how good you are, there are always people who are better. You can't be the best, and nobody gives a stuff if you're the worst. It doesn't matter. What matters is doing it! If you get to thinking, "I wasn't good enough", it's just a cop out. You're good enough, whatever you do. Just do it, and you get all the benefits.

It's all in your relationships

What's been most important to me in the past has been getting ahead, getting a name, getting a reputation, getting the job done, being good at it. Being a good Mayor, that was just hugely important. Now I've done that, and I have a name in my area of the law. I'm seen as being very successful, but what's vastly more important to me now are relationships. My relationship to my wife Candy is the most important thing to me. Having a special person in your life brings you serenity, and I feel that goes a long way towards keeping healthy.

Relationships, that's what it's about. No matter what you've got in the terms of things, or money or position, there is always someone who's got more. There's always someone of higher rank, there's always someone more important, someone more successful, with more money. If you're after a trophy wife, there's always someone with a more beautiful, younger trophy wife. You can never have the best, or be the best, or the greatest.

Some people never have enough. If you've got food and shelter and people to live with, then the quality of your life boils down to your attitude. It's what you build around you. Whether you're sitting in a palace, or sitting in a cottage, talking with friends is great. Sharing a drink and a laugh with friends is great. Snuggling up to the one you love in bed is great. The rest, as to whether it's gold or it's plastic, is really not where it's at, it's really not.

It's very trite, and it's been said many times, but when they say 'money doesn't buy happiness', that's what they're saying. It's the quality of the relationships. You can be as rich as buggery and miserable. You can have all the money in the world, and have a lousy relationship. Sure, it's hard to have a good relationship and be happy if you're broke, if you haven't got a roof over your head and you haven't got food to eat. But assuming that you can provide for the basics, then the quality of your life is all in your attitude and your relationships.

Your relationship is not like a stuffed butterfly on a pin!
I think that for most of us, if you can get that special relationship with that special someone, then that's very precious indeed. It's so precious that it's worth an enormous amount of effort. It's more important than anything else. It's really worth working on. You don't get it and just have it sit there like a stuffed butterfly on a pin, it needs work all the time. You've got to be flexible and you've got to be aware of how good it is. You've got to keep that relationship in front of you as an on-going goal. It's not like you do it, and you've done it and now you've got it, like getting an Alfa Romeo. It's not like that.
It's something that grows and changes and needs attention and it doesn't always last. You've got to look after it. If you can't get that special relationship, you can still have a great life, because you can have good relationships with lots of people.

Talk about it
I don't get nearly as stressed as I used to. I used to get really stressed, and dealt with it by having migraine headaches, and getting drunk. Now I don't get migraines and I don't get drunk. What I do is exercise, eat the right food and sleep. I believe sleep is important. Eight hours are tons, seven are good, six is enough. In addition, I talk about whatever is stressing me. I think talking it out, verbalising it, expressing it, is hugely important. Bottling things up doesn't help. Also, I'm at the point in my life where I think it doesn't matter.

When I was younger everything used to matter. Now I think it's important to talk the stress out, be aware of it, analyse it, discuss it. 'This is how I feel, why do I feel like this?' A lot of people get stressed but they don't acknowledge it and deny it to themselves. You can't do it.

Keep up with technology

One needs to keep abreast of current technology, which is moving lightning fast. Recently I enrolled in a course where I get challenged with the newest trends in everything. The partners in the firm see me as one of the few older guys who is computer literate. I want to spend more time on becoming more computer literate. I want to develop my technology skills; I've learnt to touch-type, I'm good with emails and calendar, and comfortable with the Internet, but there's a lot of more. I find getting on top, staying on top, of fast-moving technology is really interesting.

Being a lawyer keeps me mentally alert. What I do all day, every day, is highly intellectual. And apart from that, I am conscious of the feeling that it's important to keep mentally alert. I take care to be abreast of current affairs, politics, and the world scene. I've recently also taken to doing the cryptic crossword, which I find quite a challenge.

I think about everything, I think about the consequences of things, I think about Iraq, and the national economy. I love to talk to people about it and I love to listen to talk-back shows. Another challenge is taking care of my own superannuation fund, particularly with what the market has been like.

"Just do it" and "Get off it"

I have a few little phrases that I believe in. Although Nike commercialised it, I do believe in the 'JUST DO IT' philosophy. Stop the procrastination, the justifications, just get on with it and do it. But I also have the philosophy to 'get off it.' The philosophy of 'get off it', is to stop feeling sorry for yourself. Stop carrying your grudge, stop carrying on about what annoyed you, get off it and get back to being loving, friendly and happy.

Things either happen or they don't!
I have a belief in another saying, which came to me from my senior partner. He used to say things either happen or they don't, meaning don't worry about if it's going to happen or it's not going to happen. There's a lot of wisdom – we spend a lot of time getting our knickers in a knot about things that don't happen. It's better not to do that, to get on with it and just do it.

I think we all spend too much time focussed on ourselves, how we feel, what the world is doing to us, and what's fair and not fair for us. It's much better to direct your attention outwards and think about other people. Think about the people you love and what you can do for them, it makes you a lot happier. People who become self-absorbed generally seem to become less happy, not more happy. People whose attention is directed outwards tend generally to be a lot happier.

Most people don't have a particularly good life, because they don't know how to. Most people seem to be looking for happiness and satisfaction and enjoyment or whatever, externally, in things or places. My life will be good 'if only I earn x', or 'if only I marry y', or 'if only if I get overseas trips'. There is nothing wrong with all that, but it's not the source of happiness. The source of happiness is your relationships.

Because of my upbringing, what I used to value most was being right. I thought the most important thing in life was to be right, so I had to be right about everything. The second most important thing in life was money and position. It's a wonder that my first wife even speaks to me!

Maybe that is one of the advantages of getting older, because I certainly used to think that how I saw it, was how it was. Anyone who didn't see it the way I saw it, was wrong. I could be polite about the fact that they were wrong, or I could be rude about it, but they were still wrong. I don't do that any more.

Find out about your subconscious motivations

I personally believe that we all have a subconscious mind, which directs most of what we do. It influences our lives while we're not aware of it. People get into terrible trouble when what they want in their conscious mind is at odds with what their subconscious mind wants. In other words they want to do it consciously, but sub-consciously they don't. People then get into conflict, which causes mental problems and physical problems.

I think it's important to develop self-awareness, to try to find out as much as you can about what makes your subconscious tick, what it is that drives you subconsciously. Then get your life organised with that in mind, and not deny it. People deny their subconscious motivations, and try to sit on them. They get into huge conflict over them.

I believe the subconscious is probably operating at about the 8 year old level. It still believes in magic, still believes in all sorts of things. I think the more you can get in touch with it the better. (People talk about getting in touch with their inner self.)

The more you can be aware of it, the more you can get in touch with it, the more you can organise your life to cope with your subconscious needs, and your subconscious sense of direction, then ultimately you can even influence your subconscious to some extent. The result is you become healthier, mentally and physically. If you can't do that, there's lots of courses you can do, and lots and lots of ways you can approach it. If you don't, if you lack insight totally, then I don't think you're likely to ever have a very happy or successful life.

Self-awareness is absolutely essential, some ability to stand back and look at yourself, and acknowledge what you're like. Most of us in our society are brought up to believe that how we see it is how it is, that our version of what happened is the truth. People tell you what happened at work yesterday, or on the bus, or at the pub, or an argument they had with a spouse, or a neighbour. They tell you what happened as though their perception is the truth. It's not the truth. It's their filtered version. It's their perception. The neighbour or spouse give a totally different story, which is just as true as your story, or just as false as your story. Everyone's perception is different.

Many people think the world is full of bastards, and they're victims, because they think their perception is the truth. The concept that; 'My perception is only my perception. It's no more true, than your perception', is very, very helpful.

The next 20-30 years

My actuarial life expectancy at age 68 is, I think, about 78. I reckon that's short by about 20 years, and I'll live to be 100. I don't think things will be significantly different.

We've started to think about what we'll do when we get to the point where we can't swim, cycle or run. I think we'll always be able to swim, and if you can't run, you can always walk. You can probably always cycle. I can see the day will come when we can't really do triathlons any more. Who knows? By that stage there might be organised triathlons for older people who take a more modest approach to what they do. Who knows, I might organise it!

There will still be physical activity, which gives you the endorphins, which gives you the feeling of well-being and keeps you fit and healthy. The standard belief about muscle wastage being inevitable with older people is not true. In fact, older people can do weights. Older people can do most things. Another benefit is that you maintain bone density. When I first took up triathlon seriously, I went to see my dentist and he took an x-ray right around my jaw. He compared it to one two years before and he said, 'I don't get it, I've never seen this before, the bone density of your jaw has increased in the last two years'. It was a by-product of the serious exercise I was doing. My bone density generally was increasing and the dentist picked it up.

It's so wrong to say, "I'm getting old and I'm getting frailer, I won't be able to do this, I won't be able to do that. I'm going to get fat, and weak, and flabby". You don't have to do any of that. It doesn't have to be like that. The way to go, the thing to do, is keep doing what you can do. If something happens, and you can't do it any more, well, deal with that. Otherwise, I expect to be fit and active until I die – whatever brings that on.

I intend to give up the full-time practice of law and do something else, probably writing and public speaking, plus running our investments. I am also keen on writing a book, which is going to be a worthwhile contribution. I think I have something to contribute to the age-old discussion about relationships.

In the next 20-30 years I expect I'll be having lots of fun, be amongst lots of friends, especially cheerful, out-going positive people.

Enthusiasm & passion

Enthusiasm, enthusiasm for what you're doing, is vital! I was a bit of an oddity when I was Lord Mayor. I had so much passion for the job and I always felt enormous enthusiasm for the city. I love Sydney and I loved the job, and I loved the role of Lord Mayor. I was very dedicated and very fired up about it all, that's how I maintained the energy to work such long hours. I'm the same with the law, I get very fired up when I'm at work. I also think you need to be fit in order to allow your enthusiasm and passion to come out.

Live in technicolour
There was a period in my life when I wasn't fit, and I can still remember how different it was. The difference in life between being unfit, and being fit is like the difference between a black and white movie, and a technicolour movie. If you're not fit, your life is grey, and dull and boring, and unattractive. If you're fit, everything is in bright colours.

Chapter 3

Nancy Bird Walton

Nancy was born in 1915 at Kew, New South Wales. At the age of 17, Nancy became one of Sir Charles Kingsford Smith's first pupils, starting her on the path to a commercial pilot's licence in 1935 – and she went on to become the first woman to fly commercially in Australia. In 1936 Nancy entered the air race from Adelaide to Brisbane and won the Ladies Trophy.

As there were no jobs in aviation, Nancy organised a barnstorming tour and performed at country shows around north-western country New South Wales. She then met the Reverend Stanley Drummond who asked her to set up a Flying Doctor Service in outback New South Wales – a challenging and lonely career, which she had to supplement with other work.

Because there seemed little future in flying, Nancy accepted an invitation to do some promotional work for a Dutch airline in Europe. When World War Two broke out Nancy began training women in skills needed to back-up the men flying in the Australian Air Force.

In the 1950s, after a 20-year absence from the pilot's seat, she was the first foreign competitor to enter in America's famous Powder Puff Derby.

In 1966 Nancy was awarded the Order of the British Empire in recognition of her support for charities, and in 1990 the Order of Australia for her contribution to aviation and her courageous work in the outback.

Nancy is the Patron of the Australian Women Pilots Association, which she founded in 1950 and has a daughter, a son, four grandchildren and one great-grandchild. Gaby Kennard, first Australian female to fly solo around the world

describes Nancy Bird as having 'the energy of a 20 year old'.
At 88, 'dressed to kill' in suit and makeup, she spends her
life as a speaker, entertaining and inspiring others with her
aviation stories.

I get up between 6 and 8 am. I have two Vitabrits every morning, and a piece of fruit and milk. I'm a great milk drinker; I don't have tea or coffee in the morning, I have a glass of milk or calcium milk. I speak at a lot of Probus clubs – they usually meet in the morning, so that means an early departure and usually I'm home by two o'clock in the afternoon although sometimes I have to travel out of Sydney, so it could take the best part of a day.

If I have lunch at home, I usually have something like a ham and cheese sandwich or a salmon sandwich or two slices of bread and filling. I haven't eaten white bread in years, I only eat whole grains or wholemeal. I might have two eggs on toast, I'm very fond of eggs, and again I probably have a glass of milk. If I drink tea I have it so weak it might as well be hot water and milk. I don't have morning or afternoon tea, but if I'm going somewhere and I become hungry, I might have glass of hot chocolate. At home I might just put a teaspoon of honey in a glass of hot milk.

I dislike eating out intensely, because when you're a speaker you eat in so many places. My daughter's a very good cook at home. I live three floors above her and her husband, and have dinner with them every night. I usually have something grilled and salad with a potato – I'm very fond of potatoes. I love red meat, tender and red. I don't have fish very often. I'm not awfully fond of fish unless it's very good fish, or what the kids call bait. Mullet is one of my favourite fish, and that's about the cheapest fish you can buy. The other fish I like is either swordfish, or John Dory, and they're both very expensive.

I love desserts. I love Pavlova, that's my favourite, but I don't have it very often. We don't have desserts at home at all, I'd rather have a piece of fruit. Unfortunately, I do like chocolate. I enjoy a piece of chocolate at the end of the day. I don't have sugar in tea, chocolate is the only thing, and I'm devoted to honey, that's my sweetener.

We eat dinner very late, about eight o'clock, so by the time you've finished dinner and tidied up it's not far off bedtime. I usually go to bed about 9.45.

As far as alcohol is concerned, I might have a whisky before dinner as a social thing, or I might even have half a glass of wine with my family, but I don't drink very much at all. I do drink a copious quantity of water.

I take a memory pill and a vitamin pill, vitamin D, which replaces sunshine, because apparently I don't get enough sunshine. The doctor has given me half a disprin a day, which is recommended for people of my age. I take calcium tablets as well if I don't think I've had enough milk.

In the last few years I've become more conscious of food, I think we all do. When we were brought up as kids, we just ate what we were given, but I think as we get older we become interested in cooking. In fact during the war years, people became very interested in cooking because there was a limit of things to cook. Young people wouldn't have dreamt of asking you to dinner without doing all the cooking themselves. A lot of people before the war had help in the home, but during and after the war there was no help so people did the cooking themselves. I enjoyed cooking and was considered quite a good cook. It was a pleasure to prepare a dinner party and have everybody delighted with the food.

When I get stressed or tired I just lie down and go to sleep – I have the ability to go to sleep easily when I lie down. I often put a mask over my eyes and try to relax. If I can I like to have a short rest in the afternoon, but I don't do it every day. I then get up and attend to the telephone calls and the correspondence. I have quite a lot of correspondence, answering invitations etc, and that all takes time. There's a certain amount of bookwork in everybody's life and it accumulates when I'm away and that's horrifying. I'm a little shocked sometimes when I'm answering something that's six months old, but that can happen too. But sometimes it's better to reply than not reply, even if it's a year late!

I don't exercise. I do some very mild exercise, but I don't usually have much time for it. I should have a walk every day. I know what I should do. Sometimes I might go out and walk up and down the street. I know I must make a habit of doing a walk every day, about 20-30 minutes. I don't do it every day but I know I could fit it in if I was serious with myself.

I do think people should go out more, to movies, or play sport. My life is such that I haven't had the time to indulge in sport or didn't think I had the time, or I was in places where it wasn't possible. I would play tennis occasionally when I was flying out at Bourke, and see what used to be – a red telegram coming towards me. That meant it was probably an emergency and I had to take off in an hour or so. I could never be depended upon. If you made up a four for tennis and wanted me to come on a Friday or Saturday, I couldn't be sure I'd be there.

I played golf from 14 to 18, but then I went out into the backcountry where there aren't any golf courses, or where there is one, it's got sand greens. In the Manning River where I was working with my father, I had to save up to learn to fly and the nearest golf course would have been 13 miles away, with no means of transport to it. Sometimes I would hit a ball around the paddocks, and on a cold winter's morning I would swing a golf club to get warm. At school I played netball and tennis.

I had to leave school at 14 because of the depression to help my father in the country, whilst Mother stayed in the city for the education of my brothers and sisters. I had to be housekeeper and bookkeeper for my father, and I did a lot of riding. Riding was the only method of transport I had. My nearest friend was about 6 miles away, which was quite a ride.

If there's something wrong with you, go to the best person and get it fixed

I don't have any medical conditions. Everything is very good. I had a blood test recently and it is surprisingly good for a woman of my age. I get a bit of arthritis in my hands and my knees. I have two artificial hips, they're very well done and I wouldn't know I had them.

I think if there's something wrong with you, go to the best person and get it fixed. It makes sense to me. That's what medicine is all about. The doctors are making progress all the time and it's silly to put up with something like a bad hip and not have it attended to.

No matter how old you are, make the best of yourself

I accept the ageing process and try to do it gracefully and people are very foolish to not make the best of themselves, even if they are getting old. I think it's important for women to continue to dress nicely and use a little makeup to improve their looks. I remember going to a dinner given by the National Council of Women. The guests were all people over 90 and I was amazed just how many of those women not only dressed nicely, but used a little makeup. They really looked very elegant, and it was very good to see. I feel that this is one of the sad things – that women don't make the best of themselves. For some reason they think it's clever to have no makeup and to wear raggy clothes, and look a bit hippy. But I like women to look like women, and to make themselves as elegant and as attractive as they can be. I will put lipstick on just before I drive myself home, even if I'm not coming home to anyone! I put it on for myself.

I look after my skin. I am sure I didn't when I was young, I couldn't afford to, and certainly didn't know enough about it. Now I use good creams, have a massage or facial occasionally and get my hair done professionally.

I don't go out in the sun very much, I was a redhead as a child and we are not people who can take the sun. I had freckles when I was younger; the first money I ever spent on cosmetics was a jar of freckle cream. As youngsters we used to lie and sunbake on the beach. We loved to sunbake and didn't know it was bad for us. I don't even think we wore hats.

To young people I suggest you make the best of yourself. There is so much written about health now. People are very foolish if they don't observe some of it and act accordingly. To go and eat packets of chips cooked in fat, and fatty foods and takeaway foods – they're just plain silly. You've only got to see the obesity of people to know how bad it is for them. Many of them are overweight, it's sad to see.

If you're in your 40s, really make the best of yourself. Study your diet and eat the best of foods for your health. See your medico regularly and take advantage of the great facilities that we have, to grow old gracefully. There's no shortage of specialists to talk to about food, health, and beauty. Every magazine you pick up is telling you what to eat, and what not to eat.

My goal at the moment is to be a very good speaker

I speak on the history of Australian aviation. It's over 100 years since the Wright Brothers flight, which they thought was the first powered flight but actually wasn't because we just found a man who flew in 1901 in America. He was a German migrant and didn't get on with the Press so apparently it was ignored.

It was an accident that I started speaking. After the war I was asked to help with the heart campaign and I went round speaking to raise money for the air ambulance. Also I was very interested in politics and was asked to speak along with some of the politicians in order to attract more females in the audience. Then of course they brought the men along with them. Once I started speaking they recommended me to somebody else, and I suppose it snowballed. I don't charge for it, that probably makes it attractive! Lots of people charge for their public speaking, but it's my way of putting back something into the kitty.

I've been speaking two or three times a week, often flying to other parts of the state; that's too much, I lose my voice. My goal at the moment is to be a very good speaker and enjoy doing it. I get a bit over-tired these days, but I think the answer to that is to space them better. I will have to cut it down to one or two a week at the very most. The most important thing to me now is to retain my voice. I get a lot of invitations, but I am losing my voice. The specialist tells me it's just that I use it too much, and being in my late 80s, things begin to deteriorate.

In the next ten years I expect I will be dying somewhere along the way – the law of averages will do that, won't it? I don't expect one can expect to go on forever, I just hope it's quick. I don't want to be bedridden, and I don't want to lose my marbles.

Whatever you can do or dream begin it
It's a very good thing to find yourself something that you're passionate about, or keen about. Have some interest, even if it's only betting on the horses, or watching the races, or the football. It is good to have a passion about something. It might be collecting shells, or swimming, you just need to have something that you're really keen about, that's worth doing and worth following.

There's quite a good quotation that is very good for young people: 'Whatever you can do or dream begin it!' That means that if you're at school and you want to be a pilot, then talk to your teacher and make sure you take the subjects that are going to be useful to you, like physics. I've had the passion for flying since I was 12 or 13.

When I was flying 70 years ago, the idea of using a woman pilot wouldn't have been considered at any price. I had the first job that a woman ever had in commercial aviation when I flew for the Far West Children's Health Scheme. It took 20 years before another woman had a paid job in aviation – now they're flying 747's and 767's, these great big aircraft. There's something like 54 on the flight deck of Qantas and women are throughout the aviation industry, doing wonderful work. I am so proud, because we couldn't have imagined in our wildest dreams that women would ever be used as pilots.

Women proved in the war how good they could be, because they started flying little light aircraft trainers from factory to field and ended up flying twin engine bombers, pursuit planes, spitfires and all the American fighter planes. I've seen girls in civil aviation take big jobs, work their way up in the aviation industry to captains of airliners, to say nothing of the girls behind the computers and in the offices. The CEO of Mascot at one stage told me that of the 6 top executives who were responsible to him, three of them were women!

Do something, anything!

Don't just sit around at home or lie in bed! Get out, do something, take a walk to the local park and watch the people – do something, go to the shops and look at things. Go compare prices, make yourself do something. You sometimes have to make yourself do something. I made myself go into town today and I honestly didn't know whether it was going to be successful or not. I've been taking this medicine, where any tick of the clock I'd have to go to the loo, so it was a risk going to town. But I figure most places you can make a rush for a toilet. I could have said, 'I'm not well enough', but I thought, 'No, I'll get dressed and go.'

Do something; volunteer jobs, go to the hospital and write letters for people who can't write. Go volunteer to help in a nursery or something, anything you have any skills at. A lot of people as they get older go back and do what they've done as a profession, for a voluntary job in an organisation, like the Probus and Rotary Clubs. They volunteer to be a secretary or arrange the tours – please do something.

I read in the paper once of an old lady who follows the races and she only puts about 50c on a bet. But she follows the horses, and their breeding and everything about them. It's kept her alive, because she's very interested in all these things.

Bores me to death, football and cricket, but to some people it's a real passion and I believe prisoners of war in the prison camps kept themselves going by talking about who won the Melbourne cup in 1912.

I know two men who've lost their wives, years ago now, and they're still mourning them. One of them says that one day he's going to go out and lie down beside her grave and take an overdose. Another one, who leads a very busy life and was a very famous pilot in the war years, says life means nothing to him now he's lost his wife. It's so stupid that they don't want to do anything – I roused on this particular one and said, 'You go out and accept all the invitations you get. Tell everyone how wonderful your wife was and what wonderful times you had. Talk about it as much as you like. Tell people you miss her, because she was so marvellous.'

Do as you would be done by

It's very important to have that sort of integrity or principle. I don't consider I'm any role model or any example to anybody. I get a lot of acclaim and publicity, which I feel is very exaggerated; I thought that I never did anything exceptional, and I've never tried to pretend that I did any thing exceptional. I went out into the backcountry to fly because I had to fly. I didn't have enough money to fly just for pleasure. I saved up to learn to fly, and then when my father and great aunt bought me a rattle-trap aeroplane, I had to work to pay it off.

I didn't go out with stars in my eyes to help the children of the hinterland and bring an aerial medical service to the people because they needed it. I was very grateful to get a job. There was a tragedy out west where a woman after her seventh child became ill, and her husband got her to the nearest telephone on a mattress on the back of a truck. The doctor said she's got to come in, but she died 100 miles short of the nearest medical help. It was then decided to station an aeroplane to be there in an emergency. I was offered £100 for six months guaranteed work and £100 retainer. No woman had ever been offered a job in aviation, so I thought

I was pretty lucky. I had to do private work in between to make ends meet.

I didn't have finance or sponsorship behind me to be able to fly competitively. Nobody was going to finance an unknown person like myself, so I had to go barnstorming, landing in paddocks, at country shows and race meetings taking people for 10-shilling flights.

I'm not worrying about keeping myself youthful and energetic

I don't watch TV very much. I try to keep up with the news and the current affairs programs and occasionally see a documentary or some wild-life program. I think there's a lot of rubbish on TV. I listen to radio, because I think it is much more interesting.

I'm trying to learn the computer and I haven't gone completely solo on that yet, but I have a computer and my daughter insists that I keep up with it. I feel that there are a lot of women who are computer widows. People overdo the computer, they talk about their computer, they live their computers, and everything is on the computer. I think it's a bit of an obsession. I'm using it only for emails at this stage, but I'm not going to learn to use it for other things.

I don't read very much at the moment, because I have eye trouble and have to have a cataract operation. I also have a glaucoma that I'm being treated for. Although I have the sight of a 50-year old and can read the paper without glasses in the sun, I find my eyes get very sore and stingy after reading very much. I've got masses of books, 300 aviation books, although I enjoy other books. I don't read novels, but I like to read autobiographies.

I'm not worrying about keeping myself youthful and energetic, my mother was very energetic, and I think I get it naturally from her.

Apart from aviation I do know a lot about camellias, because my husband was very interested in them. I enjoy gardens and we had a lovely garden until his death.

The important thing is to have a partnership

I wouldn't marry again because I don't want to share the rest of my life. Sure it would probably be nice to be looked after, it's nice to have someone who opens the door of the car and who cares about you, but any woman has to play second-fiddle to the man she marries. You have to cut your cake to make a marriage work; it's the woman who does most of the cake-cutting and makes, we won't say the sacrifices, but who compromises.

I think the important thing in this day and age is to have a partnership, discuss things with your husband and share things, share the knowledge. They ran a wonderful program in Canada that 'Teach Your Wife to be a Widow'. So many men die, and the wife doesn't even know if there's an insurance policy. She doesn't know whether it's in her name, she doesn't know what happens. My generation of menfolk didn't take their wives into their confidence. Things are different now, wives invariably run the accounts, the stock exchange and so on.

It's information that is there for free!

There is a lack of communication between people, their children and grandchildren, because you don't see enough of them to be able to talk things over with them. I find they're not really interested in your opinions. It's a different world. They all work so hard these days, they're all so busy which is unfortunate, and they never have time to talk. I think these days you have to be busy to hold down your job and pay off your mortgage, if you're lucky enough to have one.

It is one of the sad things that young people are not interested in the experience and knowledge of their parents and grandparents. Particularly as they could tap into this knowledge and save themselves a lot of trouble. It's information that is there for free! But they'll go and pay a lot of money for a professional seminar!

I wouldn't want to impose myself upon my children in their middle age

I suppose middle age is in the 50s. I wouldn't want to impose myself upon my children in their middle age as a responsibility. I feel good retirement villages are very much better where you're with people of your own vintage and memories, and young people who are now middle-aged can enjoy their middle age, and their growing older.

I think when your mental or physical capacity deteriorates, and you know it's deteriorating; it's obvious to you. The other day I was with a woman of 80, who was still flying her own aeroplane, was as bright as a button. She flies all over the place, completely 'with it' mentally. I think that's fantastic for a woman of 80. I still drive, but I'm being a bit careful because I notice my eyes are going. But this woman was absolutely remarkable, her husband was an aviation engineer and pilot and taught her to fly. She passed all the exams and still flies to all these places. Amazing.

Somebody's certainly looking after me

They say there are no atheists in the air. Everyone who flies feels that there is a guiding hand, but just what it is, we don't know. You have close shaves and you know somebody's looking after you and somebody's certainly looking after me, because I've been exceedingly fortunate and lucky, really lucky.

I suppose I've been the subject of jealousies, people tell me I have. And sarcasm, but I ignore it. You can't stick your head out of the crowd in this country without people wanting to slap it down, can you? I think the best thing to do is completely ignore it and get on with it.

There's no point in regretting things in the past

People remind me of things in the past and I do have a pretty good memory, but there's no point in regretting things in the past. There's no point. You just make yourself unhappy. I suppose I would have been a very different person if I'd started an airline out in the backblocks. But I didn't, I didn't know enough. I wasn't educated enough to know how to manage finances, I didn't have the backing or the idea to do it. I suppose I could have made more of my life if I hadn't married, if I'd stayed a single woman and gone into the air force and been a big shot.

I'm not completely satisfied. I don't think I've led a wonderful life and done everything right, please don't think I have any tickets on myself. But what would be the point of regretting?

I feel very grateful that people still want me

I love people. I enjoy meeting people. I speak to the Probus clubs and meet such jolly nice people. They're all people who've held responsibility in the past, and made something of their lives. They have joined these clubs to continue being active, because they've retired and now have time to do things that they didn't do before. Ever since I was a kid I've enjoyed people, all sorts. I'm a people person.

I get more invitations than I can accept and I'm very humble about that. I feel very grateful that people still want me and want to hear from me. I talk about the history of Australian aviation because so few people know about it. Australians have pioneered practically every major ocean of the world by air, one way or the other, but very few Australians know about it.

This fantastic land of ours, Australia, is so exceptionally beautiful, especially from the air, and has a wonderful freedom and standard of living. I've been in countries like England, Germany and Europe etc, even America, but there's nowhere as good as Australia to live and most Australians don't realise it.

I'm a people person. People make me happy, nice people, talking to people, getting to know people, and of course this beautiful country we live in.

Chapter 4

Ron Tacchi

Ron is Italian-Irish by heritage, American by birth and Australian by choice. He migrated to Australia in 1970 following a successful career in sales and sales management in the USA.

He formed his own training company in 1973 and presented his first professional speaking engagement in 1975. Ron was among the first recipients in Australia to be awarded the designation of Certified Professional Speaker (CPS) by the International Association of Professional Speakers.

He was the founder of Australian National Sales Congress, bringing to Australia such illustrious speakers as Dr Norman Vincent Peale, Zig Ziglar, Dr Ken McFarland and astronaut Neil Armstrong. Ron was the co-founder of SWAP Australia and a founding member of the National Speakers Association of Australia. He is a Governor on the Board of Directors of the American Chamber of Commerce in Australia and actively supports many professional and community groups.

Ron is the founder and Managing Director of Speakers Network International, which is one of Australia's leading full service speakers' bureaux. At 67 he still works full time, loves walking and sailing, and one of his latest interests is hot yoga (yoga done in a heated room)!

I get up between 5.15 and 5.30am because I love the morning, and like to have a walk. I try to walk at least five days a week all year round. I do it in the dark during the winter. In the summer months, it's beautiful. It's light at 5.30 in the morning, the sun's up. But even at other times of the year when it's still dark, like this morning, it is a beautiful walk. It was great to see the QE2 coming out of the harbour with all the lights on. Rain or shine, I throw on a windbreaker and away we go. I go to sleep around 10, 10.30 most nights, and sometimes I'll stay up to midnight, but I still get up at 5.15am.

Most mornings I have fruit and some cereal, but if not cereal, I would at least have some fruit. I realise the importance of eating something in the morning, and I try to do that. If sometimes I don't eat at home I'll bring something to work with me and eat it in the office. I don't drink coffee any more, I gave that away, but I might have a decaf occasionally.

Every morning I read the paper, but I find I get really depressed reading the paper. There's nothing much of interest. It's all bad news. I had a friend that moved from the city up to the northern suburbs, he started to read the paper on the way to work every morning, and he said by the time he got to the office he was miserable. When he lived in the city he used to walk to the office, he would whistle, buy his donut and coffee and he was happy.

However I still read the paper, because in my business, it's important to know what's going on. I read the headlines, and even read the social pages quickly. In the weekends, I'll sit in bed for one to two hours and read the paper from one end to the other, every bit of it. I don't read books. I haven't read a book in years. I don't even remember reading a book. I read magazine articles, newspapers, and journals.

During the day, I graze on bits and pieces. The unfortunate thing is that we keep cookie jars at my office and that's a big mistake. I keep them for everyone else, but I'm the cookie monster! I think that if you're getting exercise and you're watching what you eat at your major meal times, then you can afford the odd cookie. If I didn't do exercise, and I didn't do weights and all the other exercise then I couldn't eat the cookies.

I usually have lunch in the office. I get invited out for lunch constantly, but for the most part I don't go out. I don't like business lunches at all. If I have to have a business lunch, I'll get sandwiches here at the office and invite the people in, so you can control when it stops and starts. Normally I'll buy lunch from a guy who comes around with a sandwich basket and he's got healthy stuff – yoghurts and salads.

Sometimes I'll bring something from home and throw in some fruit. I love fruit and eat as much as I can. I eat a lot of grapes, peaches, apples, bananas etc. In season I would eat fruit three meals a day if I could.

Dinner I love to cook, I really do enjoy cooking. I keep dinner varied, sometimes I cheat and throw in a bit of frozen with a bit of fresh, but for the most part I tend to go fresh. I'm not a vegetarian, but I don't eat fatty meat. I buy the best, best meat I can buy, everything lean. I might cook it with the fat on but then I cut the fat off before eating. I'll have a glass of wine while cooking. Normally everything is grilled, the meat's grilled and I love fish, I eat fish one to two times a week.

I don't eat much fat, and I don't eat chips. Every now and then I'll get home, and be too tired so I'll open a can of beans and cook a couple of frankfurters and I love it, but that's not every night. After dinner I might have ice cream two evenings a week, but its low fat ice cream.

I stuff myself on pizza maybe every three to four weeks, maybe even have the occasional MacDonald's or a Burger King or something like that. And I don't feel bad about it. I exercise. I know the next day I'll get on a rowing machine and I'll do a real hard workout and I'll say, "That's for the Burger King!"

I don't drink beer; I'll have two beers a month, that would be all. But I really do enjoy wine. I love wine. I would have wine probably four evenings a week, mostly red.

I take a lot of vitamins, love vitamins. I don't know if they do any good, but every day I take about eight or nine every morning with my breakfast. What I notice mostly is that I really feel good. I don't get colds, I'm regular, and so whatever I'm doing, I've got to keep doing. It's a couple of hundred bucks a month by the time you add it all up. I figure you could spend that on a dinner out, but its healthy for you. People say if you don't need it – it just goes out in your urine. Well, I feel terrific, I've got the most expensive urine in town and I'm thrilled about it.

I'm committed to exercise

I do weights about five times in two weeks, plus on the weekends we take long walks. It's not unusual to walk into the city, walk all round the city and take the ferry back. That's a good hour and a half, not a stroll, we walk, and that's our exercise.

I used to be a runner and I'd love to be running, but my knees and my ankles can't do it. I walk fast and occasionally shuffle. Every now and then I'll break into a run just to remember. I do love to run. When I was a kid, I'd get on the golf course at night time and just run. I loved it. I lived to run. I miss that, but I still enjoy the shuffle. I used to play tennis, but I kept getting beaten and I don't like getting beaten. The only sports I play are the ones I can win! I love boating, I have a boat and that's one of my favourite leisure activities.

I've just started hot yoga, which nearly kills me. Wow, is that brutal! I thought it was going to be that you pose in some position and meditate, but this is hard work. The heat at 37° is hot, very hot when you're doing things, bending and stretching. I was impressed with what poor balance I had when I started, so I know that has to improve. Also my lack of flexibility, but I know I can do it if I work on it. It's also teaching me to breathe.

Each time I go to the gym and I'm going through my routines, I keep thinking, 'Gee as I get older, I wonder if I should start cutting back on the number of repetitions, or the weight?' But at this stage I have no intention of doing that. I'm going to keep it where it is.

I think some people get old very young

I sometimes feel bad for these contact sport athletes that play a little bit longer than they should have. They end up with bad knees, bad backs and other complaints. I feel so sad for guys and gals that have big tummies and complain about back pain. There's nothing wrong with the back. It's the front. And my closest, dearest friend complains of back pain. He's got a gut and I keep saying if you'd lose your gut, you'd lose your back pain.

If I don't exercise, in 10 days my back gives me heaps, and keeps me awake at night. But if I exercise I have no problems with my back. I think a lot of the ageing process is mental, and a lot of it is acceptance. People give up doing the things that keep them young. The ability to fall down, that's a young thing, kids can fall down, teenagers can fall down, and they don't get hurt. Older people fall down, they get hurt. I think if they keep themselves fit, then they're able to fall down and they're not going to get hurt, or it's not going to be as severe.

I think a person has to think young

I think I'm about 37, so tend to play at that level, even at the gym. I see these old guys who are struggling with these weights and I suddenly realise they're ten years younger than I am! I think a person has to think young. They have to keep themselves trim enough to feel good about themselves, and this helps them age.

I worry about the ageing process, because at the end you're going to die, and I'm not really looking forward to that at all! I'm not a religious person. Maybe, I'll get religious in the last couple of hours, but at this stage I'm not expecting any big hereafter. I know this is it; there are no dress rehearsals. You don't get a second run. I really am enjoying being here, and enjoy every aspect of it.

I've never seen old fat people

My friend and role model Walter Dickman told me one time. 'I've seen a lot of old people and I've seen a lot of fat people, but I've never seen old fat people.' Eventually you have to lose weight. He convinced me of that years and years ago. I thought if I stay slim, it will increase the odds.

I enjoy speaking, running the bureau, but don't plan on doing it for too much longer. I intend to keep speaking. I've recently gotten into coaching people in presentation and other areas and I'm enjoying that. I'm thinking seriously about reinventing myself as something different. I'd love to get into comedy because I really enjoy it.

Get your health checked regularly

If something happened tomorrow I wouldn't be a bit surprised. I don't expect it to, and I'm certainly not planning on it. I'm not going to die of cancer, I just don't want any of that and I keep that out. I get tested monthly, quarterly, and half yearly. I don't want to be caught, but the heart's another matter. If I have any concerns, it would be the heart. My family history is heart, and diabetes, and I'm conscious of it.

It concerns me that my Dad was never sick in his life. Then wacko, he had a massive heart attack. Didn't kill him but might as well have. He was a couple of years younger than I am now. He was also a hyperactive 'A' type, always jumpy. He didn't die. He came home and said, "That's it!" He sold everything and moved to Florida and spent the rest of his life walking up and down the beach collecting shells. He used to make little plastic boxes and glue the shells on. I don't want to be gluing shells on plastic boxes.

Dad was in his early 80s when he finally did die. It was complications from diabetes that got him. You really don't want to have diabetes. That's bad. It takes your eyes. It rots you. They cut your legs off. You don't want to get diabetes.

In my 80s, I want to be able to maintain my lifestyle, to do the things I really like to do. I don't want to have to think twice about doing things, like going out on my boat and going to shows.

The best thing I ever did was to give up smoking

That's the best thing I ever did, and I have the worst willpower in the world. For over 20 years, I used to smoke right down to the nub – I wanted my money's worth. It took me five or six years to get over smoking and get it out of my system. There isn't a day I don't take a full breath of air, and appreciate giving up smoking. Dr Tickell said it right "You can't be intelligent, and smoke at the same time!"

You just can't smoke. Hello..... Look what it says on the pack! Go to a hospital and talk to emphysema victims. I've lost three very good friends this last year with emphysema. They couldn't breathe, only out of the top 10% of their lungs. And they couldn't talk properly. What a way to go!

Walk up the escalator

There's a reason they say stay to the left on an escalator, it's so people can go by. I walk right up there and say, 'excuse me' and they move. I don't want to wait, it takes forever, plus it keeps your bum tight if you walk up there.

I really am truly an 'A' type. I look at other people and they walk slower. They have no enthusiasm about them and there's no energy. I'd rather run than walk, and I'd rather walk fast than slow. I don't dawdle. I like to keep my eye on the person in front of me until I pass them. Then I look for the next person and pass them. I drive the same way. That's an 'A' type! My family were all 'A' types. In my family they die about now! I am exactly what you look like before you die! But mentally I'm thinking of myself living into my 80s.

You're not here for a long time you're here for a good time

My down time is anything outside of the office. It could be going on a boat. It could be walking, watching television, going to the movies, sitting talking with someone, having lunch, at the club or something. I love the weekends. Often Sunday mornings I just sit in bed reading. I love television. If I ever did get sick and had to go to hospital, the only thing I'd ask for is a private room and some earphones, and I would be fine. You wouldn't even have to come in and check on me!

I'd like to learn to meditate. People who do, tell me its'

terrific. To me it's just like sitting quietly and thinking – I do that a lot, so maybe I'm meditating already!

You should always pay yourself first
One of my strong beliefs is that you should always pay yourself first, not pay everyone else and save what's left. You should always save something for you and then do what you can. Get your investment stream set up, your property, and your share portfolio. Get yourself financially fixed. In the same exact way, get yourself physically set. Start creating habits of doing healthy things.
I believe a diet shouldn't be anything that you couldn't reasonably do for the rest of your life. I think you should start preparing your body for the long haul physically; you should start getting yourself ready. My theory is that you're born with a Lamborghini. You can't drive it around like a clapped out farm truck. If you put smoke in it, you put junk in it; you're going to hurt later.

If it's not good for you, give it up as soon as you can
If it's not good for you in the long run, give it up as soon as you can. As soon as what's reasonable. I see guys drinking too much, too long, and ending up with a big gut. It's not healthy, and your heart's got to pump through all that.
If I had a suggestion for younger people, it would be treat your physical being much like you treat your financial well-being. Plan for both, plan for the long haul. One complements the other, because it gives you pride in yourself. You feel good about yourself. I think those things are important.

Age gracefully
You can almost look forward to the ageing process because it's fun. Women think they always have to look young, they don't. I see men and women getting facelifts and they look ridiculous, like a man wearing a taupe. Get off! Why would you do that? I think you can age gracefully. If Sean Connery and Katherine Hepburn can do it, so can anybody. They

don't look like kids, but they're as attractive to other people as you'd ever want to be.

I'm very fortunate my Dad was Italian and the only decent thing he gave me was this Mediterranean skin. I can go out in the sun and I just get brown. I never looked after my skin until about ten years ago. I went to the skin specialist and he said if everybody was like me he'd be out of business!

The best way to help other people is to feel good about yourself

Most of the things we worry about never happen. The most important person in the game is you. If you look after yourself, then you're in a position where you can reach out to other people. It's the old adage – the best way to help the poor people is don't join them!

And the best way to help other people, is to feel good about yourself. I meet people in sales and they say, 'What's the key to good selling?' and I say, 'Like yourself.'

My health is the most important thing

As long as I have my heath I can do all the things I want to do. Care about yourself, look after yourself, don't let other people try to tell you who you are, what you should do. You have to use your own common sense, Get regular check ups, so that you feel good about your health. If something worries you, look after it.

I went to see a gentleman the other day at the rehab centre. He was about 54. He was fooling around on a motorcycle and now he's in a wheelchair for the rest of his life. A lovely man who still has all his faculties, but he's now in a wheelchair for the rest of his life and needs care. I don't ever want that to happen. I don't want to have a stroke, and suddenly I'm dependent on other people. So my health right now is the most important thing.

You really have to start to think about your body going the distance

Middle-aged to me would be about 50 to 55. I didn't use to think that when I was a kid. When my brother hit 40, I thought, 'The poor bugger, he's going to die any day.' And he did.

In my mid-40s I realised that I was putting it on, and I wasn't taking it off. I really got heavy. I thought, 'This is bad!' I gave up Fanta, and a lot of other things, which made a huge difference. That's about when I started exercising and getting serious about it.

My triglycerides were high and my cholesterol was high, so now every day I take medication for cholesterol and diabetes. The doctor said I'd have to take them for the rest of my life, so I accept that and take them every morning. I think exercise is like that – you can't not do it.

I notice my memory is not as quick as it used to be, but I think you can work on it. I think if you get lazy, you lose it. If you keep yourself sharp, if you play little trivia games, and you're constantly testing yourself, you keep your memory sharp. I don't think your age has to mean you lose your memory.

Old age to me now would be in your 80s, where if you haven't really take good care of yourself you start to slip and slide. People fall down in the bathtub, because they don't stay physically active. They're not flexible enough to climb in and out of the bathtub.

I see myself as a thin, older person and I see myself doing lots of things in my 80s. I can't see much past that. I don't think I'm going to be an old digger in my 90s, although when I'm in my late 80s I might!

When you hit 'middle-aged', that's where you really have to start to think about your whether your body's going to go the distance. You've got to watch your diet, you've got to start adjusting what you eat, and how often. You've got to be more conscious of the

things that keep you healthy and keep you young. Up to then you can get away with a lot, but after middle age you can't.

After 90 you're in God's power and more power to you if you can keep things going from there. That's terrific!

Chapter 5

Toni Lamond

Toni Lamond is an Australian showbiz phenomenon. She began performing as a child of ten in Vaudeville with her parents. Later she moved into musical theatre as the leading performer in musicals such as 'Pyjama Game', 'Oliver', 'Wildcat', 'Annie Get Your Gun', 'Anything Goes' and 'Gypsy'. Other shows in which she has performed include, in Australia: '42nd Street', 'Pirates of Penzance', 'My Fair Lady' – in USA, 'Cabaret', 'Hello Dolly', 'Annie', 'Mame', Oliver' and '42nd Street'.

In 1962 Toni became the first woman in the world to host her own 'tonight' show 'In Melbourne Tonight'. She branched into cabaret, taking her act to England, Scotland, South Africa, The Philippines and USA. A highlight of this phase of her career was her New York debut at the Year 2000 New York Cabaret Convention.

Toni has written three books – her autobiography 'First Half' (which was on the best seller list only eight days after release), 'Still a Gypsy', plus a cookbook. She's written several shows, including 'Full of Life', her one-woman cabaret. To assist in providing entertainment for senior citizens' facilities she has also released a CD – 'The Ultimate Sing-A-Long'.

Toni has received two Logies – the Variety Club Award for Musical Theatre Actress of the Year, and the prestigious Australian Theatre MO Award.

Toni's 72 birthday saw her travelling around Australia performing in live theatre in 'The Full Monty'! What does that say about her!!!!

I always like to have a project going, I'm an Aries. We burn very brightly for short amounts of time, the energy could light up a city and them whoooom... and you've got to rest. In my mid life, when I hit my 40s a psychic friend of mine told me that I had to make sure that I ate little and often, instead of three meals a day, to conserve my energy. When I realise my energy level is really high, I schedule things in and I've noticed in recent years that the full moon energises me and I get a lot done during the full moon.

Depending on what the day brings, I only ever sleep now for a few hours at a time. My sleep habits were broken when I got an addiction to sleeping pills after my husband died and it broke my sleeping habits forever. But I've learnt to go with that, because after I started what I call my spiritual life, I began to realise that I was getting my best ideas at four or five in the morning. That's when I get up and go to the computer and write them down quickly before they're gone. Then I'll go back and sleep like a baby for the next four hours or so.

I might be up at 6.30am getting the mind into gear for a TV interview or something. I'm a morning person anyway, because my life has been rehearsals and recording sessions, which happen early. You're usually there all day on your feet for eight hours and you get used to it. Because my projects, shows etc are always different I have no structured days. I do many and varied things. I still perform, thank God!

If I don't eat properly my energy quickly goes
I've been a tea and toast girl for years, I can't break myself of that. I'm dieting at the moment, because when they put me on cortisone I put on weight. My face blew up like a balloon and it started to affect my singing voice. On my toast I like a little bit of Provita – margarine, or I might have some honey or vegemite, and usually I have wholegrain. It was crumpets this morning, because they're not fattening without the butter. I can't give up the cup of tea with skim milk. I have skim milk and low fat foods now because my cholesterol was very high about two years ago. Now I'm used to skim and I couldn't drink full cream milk in my tea.

I used to snack myself into overweight with the ice-cream and so forth, but I'm being a good girl now, having low calorie yoghurt and eating lots of fruit. It's wonderful living near Paddy's market because I find I'm eating much more fruit than I have done in the last few years. I have found that if I don't eat properly my energy quickly goes, I lose my voice and I lose my stamina.

It is a matter of, I better eat right otherwise I'm going to lose all the things that I need to go on. I work hard when I go out and do a show. I do a 90 minute show. I don't go out and sing a bracket of three, I do an entire act. It's very hard work and if I don't eat the right stuff my performance suffers.

Now I snack on carrot straws and celery. For lunch it used to be sandwiches, but I'm not going to eat all that bread, so I'll probably do a diet drink and put a banana in it. For dinner I'll have protein and three or four veg and eat sensibly, with that a nectarine or other fruit which I find keeps me on my feet. I do take vitamin B, vitamin E, and folic acid. All those things stave off respiratory infections and bugs. But I'm also very aware that I must eat the right food as well.

For instance, the last week I flew to Melbourne at 7.45 in the morning, did two shows in a shopping centre – one at eleven o'clock, one at one o'clock – and got back on the plane at five o'clock. I came home and was at the Ashfield town hall the following morning at 9 am doing my sound check for the seniors' concert. In a 48 hour period I did three shows, and travelling. There's no time to catch a meal so you've got to really try and think ahead. You have to because nobody factors in food.

I'm eating sensibly, I grill my food, and I've cut the chips out. I am having low carbo, high protein at the moment. I find that suits me, otherwise I'm eating sandwiches and munching muffins all day long. I'm an addictive personality, terribly addictive personality, addicted to the computer, addicted to reading, addicted to this, that. I've got to really watch it. I can't have the one chocolate or the one potato chip, I've got to have the entire block or entire bag. The chocolate went right out of the diet, but if I put a teaspoon of cocoa in the diet drink it satisfies the chocolate craving.

I've become very aware of how important water intake is. I drink lots and lots of water, a litre if not more. I have a jug of water by my bed and it's gone by morning. All night long, I'm sipping the water.

With regards to alcohol, my doctor frightened the hell out of me. Because I'm on medication for this inflammatory arthritis, she said, 'You'll do damage to your liver.' I thought, 'Well, we can't have that.' I stopped drinking alcohol. I drank for years, loved my champers. We gave this party on Friday – champagne was the drink of the night and I drank water. I was so proud of myself. I'm known for my champers; as soon as I walk in, they hand me the glass of champagne!

I've still got too much to do

I do needlepoint, go to the movies, read. I inhale books. I've got books in boxes and shelves in my room, a cross between spiritual, show biz and movies. I can do acupressure and I learnt how to do shiatsu – I was doing it for the dancers in '42nd Street', running quite a business out of the dressing room.

I'm very well aware that the days dwindle down to a precious few. I haven't read every book in the library. I haven't seen every movie. I haven't written every book that I want to. I haven't sung every song that I want to. The way I want to die is to come off from a standing ovation and drop dead. But not yet, I've still got too much to do. I want to be able to write some more books and some more shows. I'd like to write another movie. I'd also like to get the movie up that I've already written with my son.

I don't want to hang around and linger around, that's too sad. I don't know how long I expect to live, because I tried to commit suicide seven times when I was in my 30s. I'm really living on borrowed time. In my 70s, every day is a precious gift.

When my husband died 38 years ago, it set off a chain

of events. I started to get addicted to sleeping pills, and the chemicals take over your body. You start not to think right. I thought, 'What's the good of it all?' and started to overdose etc. Then I woke up to myself and realised that God would say, 'No, stop it, I'm not taking you yet!'

The life I've led since then has been full to brimming over. I've started on the spiritual journey and I started to 'get it'. Hey yeah, there's stuff to do, there's good stuff happening and it's so exciting. The awards are starting to come and the recognition. It's lovely.

My mother was 64 when she died and my father was round about the same age. That was old age, when I was a child! Now of course, you're just in your prime. When I turned 64, I held my breath and surpassed my mother. My son did the same thing at 40, which was the age his father committed suicide.

The show must go on!

Everybody in show business hurts themselves. You go into the theatre and it's like being on a construction site, without a hard hat! There are so many dangers working on stage that people don't realise. There were injuries galore in Beauty and the Beast and the Lion King, chiropractic city!

I got back problems in Disney's Beauty and the Beast five years ago. I played the wardrobe in the stage show, and on my shoulders carried around a big wardrobe. It was supposed to be measured for my height etc, but it was an inch or so out and instead of my hips carrying the load my shoulders and back took it.

I was staggering with the weight, but with my training of, 'The show must go on', and my mother's training of, 'Don't complain, don't make waves'... after nine months, my spine suffered until one morning I just couldn't get out bed. For the last five years, a lot of aches and pains have stemmed from that.

I've had no catastrophic cancers or any of those things, high blood pressure, and high cholesterol yes. My father had colon cancer, which has a hereditary tendency so I have a colonoscopy every two years, and an endoscopy.

God blessed me with good skin. I haven't had any work done. I have an English skin which blossoms in damp weather. I don't go out in the sun with it. I don't smoke and I don't wash my face with soap and water. I moisturise my skin when I think of it and when I feel it's getting dry. I'm very naughty though, I don't put sun block on all the time, but I never sunbake and do make an attempt to cover up when I go out.

It slows down the ageing process

Meditation came into my life in 1990. I was writing my first book while I was doing '42nd Street', eight performances a week. In the morning I would get up and sit at the computer until it was time to go to the theatre. On matinee days that would be until noon. Then I'd have a shower and quick something to eat, and go do the matinee performance. I'd have the laptop in the dressing room, and when I came off I would type in what I thought. Then I'd go home between shows, because I lived round the corner, and I would keep writing. I was constantly for nine months doing the book, and because I'd never written a book before, I didn't know whether I could meet the deadline. It was pretty full on. I never had a social Sunday for nine months.

When I finished my book I went and had my tarot cards done, because I had a feeling that I had reached a crossroads in my life. I was living in America at the time and I'd been brought out for '42nd Street'. Now I'd written a book, I knew life was not going to be the same. My tarot card reader said 'Do you meditate?' And I said, 'No'. Meditation to me, up to that time, was the Beatles and the Maharishi, and I'd tried stilling my mind.. please....

She said, 'You should darling, you really should.' A week later, I ran into a friend of mine on the ferry coming into town. She was a singer who also did palm reading. She gave me a reading and in the middle she said, 'Do you meditate?' Well, twice in one week I figured this was a call from the universe. I thought, 'I can't meditate, I'm not good at it'. But I went to a New Age bookstore and saw these meditation tapes.

I found one called 'Through Time and Space', which was a journey to all the planets. It was an American one, and it was relaxing. You get up and leave your body there, go through a hole in the ozone and out into the galaxy. You travel to a planet and you could do what you liked there, you could populate it, or you could leave it empty, or you could do what you want with it. Then after you're getting used to that, then up you go and back into another star system, then onto another one. Then finally you came back into the room and 27 minutes had gone by.

And I said – 'Ah. Ok, now I've got it!' I was focussing on this visualisation exercise. There were no immediate revelations, but after a couple of times I began to realise that I was getting things done quicker, like the housework, making the beds, cleaning up the kitchen and getting to the writing. It was taking me about two and a half hours, now I'm doing it in 40 minutes. Now I know what they mean by expanding time.

I also began to notice that I was looking younger and that was funny, because reporters were interviewing me for my book. When I'd mention meditation, ESP, and expanding time, there would be a sceptical look on their faces. As soon as I said that it slows down the ageing process, they said, 'What!' Suddenly they were all ears. I said, 'Yes, it slows the pulse, lowers the blood pressure and I look younger now then I did ten years ago, and I've got the film to prove it!'

As Shirley McLain says, looking into a blazing fire is meditation. I found out that some men like to do the washing up, to scrub pots and pans. That's their meditation. They're focussing on a simple activity. One man said to me, 'I get some of my best ideas when I do the washing up!' Sitting watching the ocean, ironing, they become mesmerised. They're getting the meditation and not knowing it! And they're probably poo pooing it – 'All that stupid stuff'.

Miracles can happen and they do

A lot of people in show business, you'll find are spiritual. So many miracles happen to us on stage in the midst of disasters that we're quite ready to believe that miracles can happen, and they do. Miracles happen almost every day.

Meditation and looking at spiritual matters has changed my life. Now I know there's a centre and a way to get out of the stress if I'm having trouble. My main problem is learning all those songs and I keep challenging myself, we Aries do. I challenge myself with hard songs, hard word songs. I never make it easy on myself because I'm determined that I'm not going to go under due to my brain turning to mush.

I'm a great believer that if you're a writer you'd better be open to the universal mind, because that's where it's coming from. Somebody told me a wonderful story once – always acknowledge the universal mind because in that way if you screw up, it's not your fault! 'It was the universal mind that did it, it's not me!' I think it is true because I look back over things I've written and I think, 'Where did that come from? How did I know that?' It's the universal mind working through us.

Singing is good for you

I've done a sing-along CD which is doing good for a lot of people in retirement villages and aged care facilities where there's no piano on the premises. They used to sit and stare into space for days, now they can sing along to show tunes, film music, golden oldies, Irving Berlin, World War II, and Evergreens. It makes them feel good.

Singing is good for you because it releases those endorphins. That's why I was feeling so good when I was performing; I just thought I was addicted to the applause. They've had incidents where stroke victims wouldn't talk. The last thing that goes is the lyrics of a song and they start singing. People who haven't talked suddenly start singing and it can transfer from one part of the brain to another. We get letters from people saying they laugh, they smile, and they applaud for the first time.

I'm not able to do much exercise at the moment because of this inflammatory arthritis right throughout my body, but I'm going to get back into the swimming and do some aqua therapy. I come from a dancing background. When I lived in Hollywood I used to go to dance class for years, and now Tai Chi – which gives me a sense of well-being. I keep flexible because I've got to walk out on that stage. I can't shuffle out or limp out. I feel no pain on stage, the adrenalin masks it. It's magical.

I'm so lucky I have many wonderful friends

I value my friends the most. I have wonderful friends. I've been able to keep friends; from the little girl I used to play with next-door when I was seven. I'm so lucky, when I saw how many people came to my 70th birthday party – a two-day celebration. Being surrounded by friends keeps you going!

My son is very important to me. It's golden. We write together. We don't talk to each other like mother and son. When I look around at some children who aren't speaking to their parents I think, 'How lucky am I, how lucky.' Tony and I respect each other's opinions, we're on the phone, we're giggling, we talk in code, we've got that wonderful code that people in families have, and we often both end up falling on the floor laughing.

In a hundred years this won't mean a thing!

I do live a stressful life. The stress is good for me for the opening night of a show, because that gets the adrenalin pumping. For the longest time I never slept the night before the opening of a show and I would be exhausted. It took me a long time to figure out that the adrenalin would kick in to compensate. Eventually I just stopped worrying about that; 'You're not going to sleep the night before a show. You're going to lie in bed. You're going to obsess over the words and you'll obsess over how you're going to look.' It all goes with the territory.

I have a few sayings. 'It'll be right on the night' is the theatrical one. It better be right on the night! I think my Aries optimism saves me every time. My sense of humour and being able to laugh is terribly important. In my act I do a lot of comedy to make people laugh, because I want them to go out feeling good from seeing me. I want them to go away feeling, 'I didn't think about my troubles, for the last hour or so'.

When you're in your 20s you need to take care of yourself. You feel as if you're invincible. I was at every party. I was having success in show business. My name was up in lights by age 24. I went out to all the parties and I was drinking champagne. I was staying up all night, burning the candle at both ends. There is a price to be paid at the other end, when the joints begin to go.

My suggestion is to take care and look after the basic habits of eating. I worry about the girls that go out on Friday nights and get off their face. That's a culture that we didn't have. We got drunk, but it was in the safe environment of a party with our friends. These kids, who go into pubs and end up reeling around the streets. To my horror they're now putting things out on the market to stop people spiking your drinks. They're putting themselves out there, and they're in danger.

I think that spiritual belief really helps you, because it centres you. When things start to go crazy, you realise you haven't meditated for a while. The world is getting progressively madder, like loud pounding music coming out of dress shops. It must drive the assistants nuts working there all day. There's no peace, and quiet and you've got to have that.

In my 50s I realised that I didn't really need someone else to make me happy. That's when I started to write, started to travel, started to do most things. I don't have to ask anybody's permission – and I'm doing a song in my act now which so many people can relate to. Now I'm living alone and I like it. When I lock up my apartment, I've got all the keys. I'm living alone and I like it. Boy oh boy, what a full life I've got! A terrifically full life.

Without health you've got nothing

Health, I value the most, good health. That's the apex of everything. Without that you've got nothing. The brain never stops. I have all my own teeth, thank you. I've been wearing glasses for reading since I was 14 and I can't read the small print now, like almost everybody I know, but have glasses I bought from the chemist.

The days are dwindling down to the precious few, and I want to fill them. Possessions aren't it. Friends are it, but I must have always known that. I love pretty things and shiny objects. Let me tell you, I'm Miss Sequin. But if I lost them, well I'd just go on. I'm not earthbound with objects.

I suppose I'm in old age, I don't know. I don't think so, the barrier keeps moving. Somebody who was 70 when I was younger was; 'God they're old!' If you looked at most of my friends, they're all younger than me, so I must be old! I have scads of chums who invite me out to dinners and a lot of the gay guys. A lot of my friends are younger and speak to me on their level.

Aries are much younger, it's the vitality and the energy. Always wanting to know something new. The pioneer of everything. I was one of the first with an answering machine in Australia, when you had to lease it, you couldn't buy it. That was back in the late 60s. I've got to be the first to have anything, like the first colour television.

I learnt to use the computer in 1986 – I was in my 50s and I didn't have a job for five months when there was a big strike in Hollywood. I went to work for my sister who had an Apple. I've now written tons of stuff on the computer, but I still can't talk the jargon.

Keep interested

The way to keep mentally alert is to keep interested. I'm very lucky my brain works overtime at times, thank God.

I'm interested in everything. I read everything. I watch everything, even if I don't like it. I like to read or turn the television on to see what is happening in the world. It's important for me to know what the latest trends are, because it's useful to me in my comedy writing. I know what I'm sending up. It's grist for the mill.

It makes another joke form. For example, I was talking about reality TV and the first Big Brother had just finished. I said, 'All the years that I rehearsed, learned words, learned songs, had dance lessons, worried about my weight, and went to the hairdressers to become a star, when all I had to do was put on a pair of bunny ears and learn to bum dance!' That's a gag that's immediately recognised. I said, 'How show business has changed. Last year Tom Hanks', big movie Castaway lost millions, people stayed away in droves when they found they couldn't vote him off the island!'

You've got to know what's going on out there. That keeps you young. I hang out with younger people. A lot of people aren't comfortable with that; 'Oh I wish we had the old days.' What's the point of that! The world evolves and it changes. We don't have what we had before but it revolves – it comes back in another form.

Follow your heart. Don't die wondering.

Follow your heart in what you want to do, don't let people stop you, because there's always people round you saying, 'Oh, don't be stupid! You can't do that!' or 'When are you going to get a real job? (I'm talking about the artistic side of it now) Follow your heart. Don't die wondering. I'm not going to die wondering. I've tried just about everything that's legal. I know what its like to write a book, I know what it's like to get up on stage. I know what its like to make a record. When they told me I couldn't make a record, I went out and financed it myself. I'm in my third pressing and it's still selling! I learnt not to take no for an answer.

It also makes you feel good inside if you can do something for someone else. Maybe one day a week I do meals on wheels or go on Christmas day to help prepare a meal for the homeless. I speak a lot to Probus Clubs – I look at it as putting back what I've taken out. Do it!

Someone in their 40s is now looking at the second stage of life. They've probably shed their first partner. They may have found that a certain lifestyle doesn't suit them and be looking around to taking up what they didn't do when they were 20.

DO IT! It's never too late. Even someone in their 60s – the same thing, IT'S NEVER TOO LATE! Take up needlepoint, painting, singing, dancing. Do it! Whatever makes you feel good.

Follow your heart and take care of your health.

Chapter 6

Colleen Wilson-Lord

Colleen Wilson-Lord OAM was the State Director of the Senior Adult Unit, NSW Department of Health, from 1983 to 1991. She has successfully developed national healthy lifestyle programs such as Walking for Pleasure, Gentle Exercise, Aqua Fitness, and Vacations for Pleasure, and is currently promoting Nordic Fitness Walking and a new sport for seniors – Lifeball.

Colleen was on the Board of the Australia New Zealand College for Seniors for nine years, her educational programs covering Australia, Norfolk Island and Fiji. She lectures on pre-retirement planning for major companies and conducts Recreation and Wellness programs including a memory-training program called "Fending Off Forgetfulness".

Colleen acts as a consultant to numerous government and tertiary bodies including NSW Department Of Health and NSW Department of Sport and Recreation. Amongst many positions, she is a Board Member of the Sport and Recreation Industry Training Advisory Board, Vice President of Age Concern, Albury, NSW and committee member NSW Rural Falls Injury Prevention Program.

Colleen's dedication to her work has been recognised with many honours and awards including the Order of Australia Medal, Advance Australian Foundation Award and the Lifetime Achievement Award for the Australian Fitness Industry.

Where does Colleen find time to sleep? At age 65 she is tireless in her mission of spreading the health message to seniors. She also teaches Gentle Exercise, Water Exercise, Tai Chi for Arthritis, Nordic Fitness Walking and...still manages to find time to be with her husband and grow her own vegetables.

I get up between six and seven, depending on what I have to do for the day. I like to go to the swimming pool. However if the weather is too cold I like to do other exercises like Tai Chi. I find I must do stretching every morning to help prevent me feeling so stiff. I have a quick shower and have breakfast, which is cereal with psyllium and fruit, two pieces of wholemeal toast, and a mixture of different juices made fresh from the vegetable garden.

Usually the phone starts ringing at 8.15am but I try not to answer it until 9 o'clock and then it's full on for the rest of the day, either working from my home office or driving fairly long distances to my appointments. At the moment we're in drought and it's very difficult fitting home duties in with my consultancy business, as my husband Brian and I have to spend a lot of time saving water (in buckets) to put onto the garden. We hope for everyone's sake we have some decent rain soon.

I always try to have some morning tea, about mid morning to keep my blood sugar levels up. I have a piece of fruit or a wholemeal biscuit with a cup of tea. I don't have as much tea and coffee as I used to and I find green tea very beneficial. I don't keep sweet biscuits in the house as they are too tempting and we really only have them on special occasions.

If I'm at home at lunchtime I'll make a salad, raw carrot, raw vegetables, etc out of our garden. If I'm out, it's a sandwich, as this seems to be the most convenient. At night we have a standard meal with as many vegetables as we can. We've become fish-eating vegetarians and eat a fair bit of fish when we can get it. Vegies and stir-fries, with red meat about once a week. No dessert other than fruit, which we both enjoy. I have found a beaut recipe for dessert which is so easy and fat free. Yes, poached pears. Quite yummy.

I try to have nothing fried. When we go out for a meal, I might have something with a few chips. I never feel guilty about this, as it's like a treat. I never eat pizza, not even tempted.

However sometimes I have a hamburger, if I'm driving long distances and need to stop for a meal. Sometimes the variety of food offered is limited so I go for a steak sandwich or a hamburger. At least you get some salad – and if you ask for no cheese, it reduces the fat intake. Eating at take-away places like Diners when you travel alone at night is really the best place to go for a meal as it is safe and you can usually find something suitable if you look hard enough.

I drink lots of water and have water in the car all the time. I drink at least three water bottles a day. I have learnt that drinking more water is really necessary. I'm trying to practise what I preach. I also have water on my bedside table and drink it if I wake up in the middle of the night. I believe drinking lots of water keeps you regular and I've certainly proven that.

As far as alcohol is concerned, I really do enjoy a glass of chardonnay. Whenever we go out for dinner I like to have a chardonnay, but at home we don't have wine unless we're having visitors. The reason we don't have wine on a regular basis at home is I feel it could become a habit that's too easy to fall into. Anyway, wine is a relaxing social activity and I try to keep it to just that.

What goes into the body, is going to be what shows on the outside

I firmly believe that what goes into the body, shows on the outside. I really believe it's the food we put in our bodies that gives us energy and feeds the whole system. I think that the food today is not very fresh and has so many chemicals. Our body is wonderful at being able to maintain itself, but because our food does not have all the nutrients we need, I believe supplementation is important so I always have additional vitamins that have been prescribed for me by my General Practitioner.

Recently we've been growing our own vegetables. We don't spray anything and the bugs and the bees have a wonderful time, but I know when I go down and pick something out of the garden that I'm getting purely what's in the soil. It's a great feeling.

I've been under an ortho-molecular specialist for many years and have a lot of supplements that I enjoy taking. He's kept me going through my many health challenges and his knowledge is so fantastic. I firmly believe that if you need to take a vitamin supplement, they should be given on the advice of a specialist in that area. I have a range of well-programmed vitamins and antioxidants suitable for my body. I take glucosamine and chondroitin sulphate for my arthritis and a whole range of things, for joints, muscles, the mind as well as a liver stimulant.

As far as stress relief is concerned, I do relaxation exercises every morning before I get out of bed. For five minutes or so I try to relax my whole body and visualise the day. I do this again at night before I go to sleep, with a relaxation tape or relaxing music. My husband and I enjoy walking together, outdoors, preferably in the forest, and I love bird-watching.

I also find the garden is very relaxing. Sometimes I go out to a little spot in the garden and do Tai Chi, the lotus program, 15 movements. I practise this program until I feel I've unwound and really enjoy that. I also teach Tai Chi for Arthritis, so that helps keep me relaxed.

I love teaching aqua fitness. Sometimes at the end of a busy day, I drag myself there, thinking, 'Why am I doing this? I've got too much on'. As soon as I hit that water I'm a different person. Even though I might be exhausted, it just takes away all the stress. It brings me life and I find the water very calming for me.

I do everything that I feel keeps this body going. I do light weights and dyna-bands. I used to have a personal trainer for six to nine months, and have found half an hour of intense weight training very helpful. In the summer I'm in the water every second day, teach aqua fitness four nights a week in three different rural towns, and sometimes I'll walk in the afternoon. Occasionally I also teach an introduction to Tai Chi on a Saturday afternoon.

I'm also promoting this new sport Lifeball and am involved in training the trainers. It's very exciting – I have a passion for team games, and I think that as you grow older you tend to isolate yourself. This is a walking game, based on netball or basketball, and can be walked at a very fast or a very slow pace, depending on the person's ability. It improves co-ordination, balance, reflexes, and strength and is going to be part of a big falls prevention program for the Department of Health. We're also introducing it into schools. If you're not good at sport, this is the sport for you.

We should be more aware of mental health

As we grow older I definitely think we should be more aware of mental health. I don't think it's because we become unable to improve our memory, I think a lot of it is because we try to do too many things at once. We get a bit overwhelmed with too many things on the one day. If we leave things behind we give ourselves a very hard time and put it down to age. I think a lot of it is to do with organisation and being more alert.

I read a lot, I really enjoy music and I enjoy singing around the house. I also think that living with a husband who is extremely intelligent, and who does cryptic crosswords all day has kept me mentally alert. Crosswords don't work for me – it's meeting stimulating people, and not isolating myself that has kept me on my toes. My work also keeps me mentally stimulated.

If you start to feel old and think you're old, you are

I don't feel any different from when I was younger. If you start to feel old and think you're old, you are. I'm positive that everyone feels 15 years younger than they are. I feel 20 years younger. I don't feel much different to what I did in my 40s.

Middle-aged is what you want it to be, for who you are. Theory tells us middle aged is about 40 to 45. That's what they tell us, and old age is anything over 55.

Well, that went out. I talk to people about old age and I'm much older than they are now. I never thought that would happen. It only seems like yesterday that at my pre-retirement seminars I was the youngest presenter. Now I'm often the older presenter and I'm talking to people much younger than myself about planning for retirement, planning their lives, talking about good health. Personally I don't try to think about my age at all.

I can see the differences in my body and I can see the differences in the outside covering and I know all the differences are there. But I honestly and truly feel I have as much energy now as when I was 40. Then I was carrying a lot more baggage around. I feel I can keep up with most people in the workforce that I consider to be much younger, like the students that work with me who often say, "Can we go away and have a rest because you go too hard!"

I think elderly now is well and truly over 80. I look at people now who are 70 and they're out there having a wonderful life. They may not have much money, but a lot are in good health. If you're in good health when you're 70 or 80, then you have an opportunity to get the best out of your mature years. I think old age is when you start to deteriorate and become less able-bodied and that could be at 80 or 90.

Don't let your numbers dictate how you're going to behave and how you're going to live the rest of your life

I know I'm 64, but I don't' feel that way at all and I don't want to be around people who tell me that's what I've got to be. -'You've got to slow down now you're 64!' I love being around younger people, no I'll rephrase that. I really love being around vital people, I don't care if they're 88 or 17 as long as they have a good attitude to life. They get up and have a go, so don't let your numbers dictate how you're going to behave and how you're going to live the rest of your life.

My health is the most important thing to me, mental,

physical and spiritual health, because if I'm in good health then I can handle all the other wonderful things in my life, like my husband, my family, and my extended family, who I love very much. I don't care how poor I am, as long as I have good health.

In my 20s relationships and work were important. Being in love, and having a good family life and enjoying my work. Enjoying my work has always been a big thing for me, otherwise I wouldn't be out on the road like I am at my age. It's a huge driving force. What I achieve is very important to me, but without my health I wouldn't be able to do any of it.

In the next 20 years I want to continue running my own business. It's pretty hard, but I've achieved some great things and I want to continue to do that. I want to get Lifeball out there to as many people as possible. I will cut back, but I want to continue to run my seminars, and be out there giving the messages and preaching the gospel about health and wellness and feeling good about growing older. I want to continue to be a pioneer in what I do.

I'm working with Vietnam Veterans at the moment, which I'm really enjoying. Working with men in that environment is very interesting and challenging and has given me another new purpose. I have started to introduce them to Nordic walking that has involved me in a new exercise routine. It's easy and so beneficial. Wish I had started this type of walking years ago.

I don't think we understand enough about each other
My advice to people under 30 is, don't burn the candle at both ends too often, and try not to fall in love too many times! Broken hearts can be so hard to handle at any age. You can never tell anyone how to run their life, and relationships play an enormous part in how you deal with your life. 90% of us look for a partner and think that's going to make a difference in how we want to continue on for the rest of our lives. Unfortunately, with the divorce rate the way it is

and relationships moving in and out, this isn't the case. Our family structures are not going to be the same in the future, and I think its terribly important for young people to learn how to compromise, how to live in relationships, and how to get the best out of each other.

That is something that's missing today. I don't think we're patient enough. I don't think we understand enough about each other, and really get to know what kind of person we want to live with and that could be just flatting with somebody. Good relationships don't just happen.

Don't stay in relationships that are dragging you down

Don't stay in relationships that are dragging you down and mentally disturbing you. If your life isn't happy, try and sort it out. Do everything you can to make the relationship work – if you can't, move on. If your family life and your personal life are not happy it will affect your health, and it will affect the way you conduct yourself and how you feel for the rest of your life.

Get as much support as you can, go out there, find out about yourself, who you are, what you're doing, and why you're doing it. Don't sit around all day over a cup of coffee telling everyone how sad you are and how bad everything is – get up and start to find out why it's happening. A lot of anxiety we bring on ourselves. We have to find the right environment to live in, and in a lot of cases that might be living alone and having friends outside.

I really think 40-50 is a really vital time. From 40 onwards, your body does start to change in many different ways, and it's the time in your life when you really must start to look after your mental, physical and emotional health. It's the time when you need to put the good fuel into the engine. If you don't, then it really comes against you in your 50's and 60s.

If you're in a relationship at 40-50 and you have teenage children, it's the one time when you really need to stop and say, 'Where is my partner? What's been happening to us?' It's a critical time when you sometimes drift apart. It's vital that you find the time and the money to have weekends away; meals out together on your own, away from the kids. It's time to find time for the relationship, to try and not focus on the kids as if they are the only things in your life. I have learnt that children are only on loan, and that we have to deal with the day when they will be out on their own and we are left with just us, or perhaps just one.

Whatever you've got left make the most of it

I moisturise my skin everyday, wear sun block all the time, and feed my skin – because I think good skin comes from internal health as well. I've had some skin cancers burnt off, which has been frightening. When I was a teenager my mother was always telling me to wear a hat, but the skin cancers have been on my legs. I think now perhaps I only really worried about my face and probably didn't think as much about my legs.

Don't get too worried about the wrinkles that come. You see them and you think, 'There's another one'. I have thought, 'Would I have a face lift, or something similar?' At one stage I thought. 'Yes I would love to have something done with my neck'. (I hated having a craggy neck) But now I know that I wouldn't put myself through another operation.

I think you've got to look after your skin. Unfortunately, a lot of women don't wear any foundation or any moisturiser and I feel it's important to feed the skin, and to look after the skin and to make the best of whatever you've got. I think whatever you've got left, make the most of it.

Sexuality is a big issue

I have gone off hormone replacement therapy, which I felt I had to do on the advice of four different practitioners. As a result I certainly have noticed a change in my body shape and changes in other areas. It was another area I had to take control over. When I went off hormone replacement, and I'm saying this for other women, the thing that really threw me was that I didn't think I would experience so quickly a lack of sexual stimulation. I was concerned that I was the only one that suddenly wasn't physically active in that area, owing to the atrophy and dryness in the vagina.

I have become an expert at finding out everything about how you can continue to have a normal sexual life dealing with all those problems. Some medications work and some don't. It is a big issue for healthy women who want to have a normal healthy sexual life as they get older. I have many friends who want to re-marry or want to have new partners in their 60s and I don't think there's nearly anywhere near enough information available to us.

Sexual health is one topic I speak about in a lot of programs. Sexuality is a big issue, and I've also learnt so much about men and their problems – how medications impact on their sexual drive and performance. A whole range of things need to be discussed openly to make people more comfortable about where they are sexually. There's many things that are normal for you to be involved in, rather than making you think that, 'Oh well, there's no point, it doesn't really matter.' Men are also suffering, feeling that they are incapable of having the sex life they had before. We need to look at what your sex life is going to be now. There are other ways we can help to stimulate each other and be close to each other and have a normal relationship.

A lot of older men don't go on into a relationships because they're frightened that it's all to do with erection and it's not to do with companionship, love and tenderness. A lot of women don't go into those relationships either, because of the dry vaginas and their worries about sexual performance. People need to feel good about everything that's happening to them.

I've had deep vein thrombosis and a pulmonary embolism, and I also had a car accident which left me with a dislocation in the right shoulder and spinal injuries and I still get a good deal of pain on the right hand side. I've had many breast scares, lots of problems with cysts in the breast and I'm always under observation.

How do I deal with these medical challenges? It's important for me to have mental satisfaction and know what it is I'm up against. It's being an active consumer of healthcare. I regularly go and have checkups, blood tests, pap smears etc and I look after myself and just get on with it. It's really important to have a positive attitude. You've only got to look around and there are so many other people worse off than you are.

You've got to forget old heartaches

You've got to forget old heartaches. Don't look back on the past, other than perhaps the good times. Don't wallow around in the pain of the past. I believe a lot of those painful experiences affect you emotionally, and to continue on you have to take charge of those feelings. I think being a forgiving person is a great benefit to health. My philosophy of life is to live and let live, and to look to the future and always surround yourself by like-minded people – people who are like you, and who you get something from, and they get something from you.

Fill your life up with as many people as you can that make you feel good. Surround yourself with people that have the same values, as you have and who stimulate you and make you feel important. I think that feeling valued is a very important part of how we deal with growing older. To feel valued you have to give a lot of yourself to other people, and have a great deal of tolerance of others – especially your friends, family and colleagues.

To feel you have contributed to supporting someone helps keep you feeling younger which enriches your self-esteem. My philosophy as I grow older is to look at life as a tapestry full of many different textures, which represent life's achievements and problems. As we grow older we can finish off the tapestry with some good strong fibre and colour (living to the full, not giving up). When finished we will feel a sense of achievement that will satisfy us for the rest of our life.

I live just for today. I think around 80 would be nice to achieve, as long as I'm still productive and can manage to look after myself and look after whatever family I have around me. I think it's important you make each day the best day. To put your best into it, and I tell all my close friends and family, every day, that I love them.

Chapter 7

June Dally-Watkins

In 1949 June-Dally Watkins was Australia's 'Model of the Year' and declared 'the most photographed model'. She then, encouraged by her mother, set about establishing the first Personal Development School in the southern hemisphere. She also pioneered Australia's first Model School and Agency, and most recently Australia's first Business Finishing College. June still has a passion today for helping young people grow and flourish, and works tirelessly.

She has led an exciting and challenging life. Born an illegitimate country girl at Watson's Creek in New South Wales, she ended up on the catwalk at a Hollywood poolside party for Marilyn Monroe, and had a romance with Gregory Peck.

June is Ambassador-at-large for Crossroads International and has taken humanitarian aid to Croatia and Bosnia. She has been awarded the Order of Australia for her commitment to business, and in 1998 was selected Australia's Most Inspirational Business Woman by the Australian Business Women's Network.

June doesn't want to admit to herself or anyone else what her age is, but her business has been going for 55 years now, and she started at 22, so you work it out!

I'm an early riser, awake and up by about 6, 6.30am. I'm a very light eater for breakfast. I eat All Bran with fruit; milk sometimes, usually Soya milk, which I like very much. I used to have toast, but now I'm more into cereal and a cup of tea. I try to avoid coffee as much as possible. For a time I was very much hooked on cappuccino – I would bring one to the office or have one sent up in the middle of the morning or while we had a meeting.

I've just come back from holidays feeling fit and healthy, so I've cut down cappuccinos, and I'm really taking extra care not to have too much caffeine. I'm just feeling so wonderful since I had a complete holiday, rest, exercise and all those good things you can do in Bali for two weeks – body massage, facial, manicure, cream bath for my hair and shoulders. It was so good. Early to bed and swimming every day in the pool.

I start the day very early, because I usually get into my office by 8.30 in the morning. I work very hard and have huge demands on my time and energy. The business is a very 'full-on' school and the students like to spend time with me personally. I'm always thinking up new courses to run, new things to do. My mind never stops.

I bring my lunch to work, which is usually made up of good wholesome things like salads. My aim is to be home now before five and go to the spa where I do my exercise. Then I go to my apartment, make a light meal and have an early night.

What we eat is what we are

My light meal might be pasta, chicken and vegetables, and from time to time it will be a small steak with vegetables. I try to eat fish two or three times a week, which I always grill, or boil. I never fry anything and I don't make sauces. Even though I live alone, I love cooking, reading recipe books and making exciting dishes, which are all healthy.

When I go out I have fish for dinner, or something light. When I'm with friends, I may have a glass of preferably red wine with dinner, but I have an old fashion outlook with regards to having red wine with more robust foods, rather than light foods like fish.

I don't eat between meals, and I try not to eat much bread. I have Vita Wheats, Weetbix and things like that instead. I have never drunk aerated drinks like Coke, Pepsi, or those flavoured mineral waters.

My whole life, I've always been incredibly aware of the food I eat and have always eaten well. If I go overboard and eat something rich, fattening and wonderful like a blueberry cheesecake, or chocolate cake with walnuts and lots of cream, then the next day I will eat very little. I have always felt that balancing my intake of food was very important, and I'm a great believer that what we eat is what we are.

I go to bed early, I believe in sleep – it's the greatest way to rejuvenate and refresh ourselves. I like to go to bed between 9.30 and 10.

As well as keeping our body active, we must keep our mind active

I have been working for the last two years under tremendous pressure, because the principal of my business college developed a brain tumour, and my General Manager accepted a job to go to New York to train new teachers. I came back and started running the business again myself, so I have been working incredibly hard. But I'm a worker and always will be.

I like to work hard, and pray that the Lord will keep me healthy and keep me sensible, physically fit and mentally alert, so I can continue to work for a long time. I would love to keep on being busy in my business, for as long as I possibly can. I have no intentions to retire. My brain must be challenged every day, as I believe this is incredibly important. As well as keeping physically fit, I want to keep mentally fit and I know that running a business means being challenged constantly. I have seen too many men and women give up and then just go straight down hill.

When I go home in the evening, I go to the spa and exercise there. This includes exercise under the shower, shoulder and waist exercises, and walking on the spot. I'm a tremendous believer in walking. I walk to and from the office and walk very fast.

Now that I live in the city, I don't have a car and I don't want a car. I don't want the hassle of having to park. I love public transport. I pretend that I'm a visitor, a tourist in Sydney, and I do what I would do if I was in Paris, Rome or London. I walk everywhere, I don't take cabs, I walk to catch a bus, go by ferryboat or catch a train, and when I get there I walk to where I have to go. I believe every day that people must go out and walk briskly.

I used to be a tennis player and a swimmer, but now I don't have time due to working five to six days a week. We have classes all day on Saturday, so I usually come in and spend time with the students. I love watching their progress and encouraging them. Sundays I may meet friends, or will work at home and go for a walk. Sometimes I go down to Chinatown and Paddy's Markets and buy fruit and vegetables, but I'm always busy doing something active.

When I'm stressed I go down to the spa and kick my legs, relax and think. I have a very good rapport with myself. I can talk to myself and encourage myself to relax. I say, 'Hey, this isn't going so well, watch it! Be aware.' I talk to myself a lot.

Also to relax, I go home, pick out a recipe book and read it. I love to read but I don't have a lot of time. When I read a book I can't put it down, so it absorbs a lot of my time. I don't want that too often, so I just pick out a recipe book, sit and look at the pictures, read the recipes and think, 'Oh I'll cook that,' and I never do.

I don't meditate, do yoga, or stretching, although I did yoga for a while with Roma Blair years ago. I always laugh when I remember visiting friends on the Gold Coast, when they had those houses with fibre-like walls, and I was showing them how I could stand on my head. I put my arms against the wall and flung my feet up and went straight through into the next room. That was the end of standing on my head.

I think you are as old as you think you feel

I had this wonderful Aunty; she lived until she was 94. My grandfather lived until he was 92, my grandmother 87, and they were incredibly fit and well. They lived in the country and were hard workers. My mother died at 74 of cancer of the pancreas, but I believe it's our mental attitude.

I don't want to admit to myself my age. I don't deny the age I am, I just don't think about it. I don't want to think about it. I don't want age to become a primary importance in my life, because I feel I am absolutely the same as this wiz kid Sally, a fantastic young ambitious woman who works for me. I think that I'm absolutely equal with her. I know I'm much smarter than a lot of young people who come to my college and the teachers. I know more, I'm more attuned, more alert than they are, but if I started to think old, and think my age, I might talk myself into it. I don't ever think age, I don't say my age; if somebody asks, I always say 25. I don't want to act like a teenager, or dress like one, I prefer to be a dignified woman.

I take care of my skin, I use a cleanser, day cream, night cream and I would never go to bed with makeup on. I also know that if I'm healthy on my inside it will reflect on my skin. I've always encouraged our students to use a body lotion and take care of their skin, brush their hair, and brush it often. 'Keep it alive,' I say to them, you don't just brush your hair, you brush your scalp as well.

I try not to go out very much in the sun, just a little bit. I love the winter sun, but I try to avoid the summer sunshine. It is such a pleasure to sit and walk in the winter sun, as it warms the soul. If I do go out in the summer, I always use sun block. It's sad that some people think brown is beautiful, that if you're not brown you're not beautiful, and they will go out in the sun and just lie and lie and lie.

What we are is who we are

My children say, 'Mum we like you as you are, don't ever have a face-lift because then you would look like something you're not.' Everybody knows when someone has had a facelift because it gives them a very stretched, unnatural look, and it seems difficult to smile. Eventually they sag and wear out in time. Again, I believe we should be pleased with ourselves. What we are is who we are. It reminds me of those years ago when photographers would re-touch a photo. They would take a photograph of someone, re-touch the lines out and re-touch the character out. I'm proud of my lines! I've earned them!

I don't have arthritis, thank you Lord. I don't have anything wrong with me. I had my thyroid removed 42 years ago and that's all! I grew up in the thyroid belt, up beyond Tamworth, where many thyroid problems came from. As a consequence I have to take Thyroxin. All my friends are popping pills, but I don't take anything other than Thyroxin. I'm afraid that if I take something, it might have a bad effect on me. I'm doing fine, thank the Lord. I feel great.

I love to be naturally high on life
People should love themselves, not in a vain way, but they should be the custodians of their body. They should love it, take care of it, and hope and pray that it's going to last them to a very healthy maturity. I'm not going to say old age! It's important to have the right attitude and they must be very aware of their exercise regime and what they eat and drink. I've never had time to go to the gym, but I'm very aware of keeping my body fit and in good order. While we exercise our body, we have to keep our mind exercised too. I work and I challenge myself every day.

I am so much against smoking. I'm totally against it. Smoking is so damaging to one's health. I have a glass of wine occasionally and even love a glass of beer from time to time, if I'm thirsty and it's hot. But I think that drinking too much is also a great danger to one's health and one's mind. To think of drugs or smoking those funny cigarettes, or taking anything synthetic into our body – I'm very much against it. I love to be naturally high on life.

I know somebody who said, 'I would rather die five years younger than give up smoking, I like it so much!' She won't accept it is a drug and she is hooked. Her body craves it, a true addiction, and when combined with excessive alcohol consumption I believe it to be a lethal combination destroying body and mind.

Sometimes, when I think I've been having too much of the good life travelling, or having too much pasta with my daughter in Italy, then I just cut down. I have one of those kinds of bodies. If I eat a lot, or I'm not aware of what I'm eating, I will start to put on some weight, not much but I will notice it. Then I just change my regime, cut down and it goes straight away. I can put it on in a day, and take it off in a day. It's important not to eat because you're miserable or depressed, but to be mentally aware. To be physically attuned, and mentally aware.

I believe you have to love yourself

People have to look after themselves. They can come here, to one of our programs and we will show them what to do. I just can't understand why people can't do it for themselves. Eat well, be sensible, get out there, walk, and live an active life.

I believe you have to love yourself. That means you have to respect yourself and take care of yourself. I'm a great believer in love. I think you have to love everybody around you. When you love and like yourself, it is easy to love others, and it's easy to accept love from other people. If you surround yourself with love and friendship, that saves you from getting bitter. Lonely people are bitter. If people are bitter, they drive their friends away and they forget to smile and be warm and friendly. People go away from them, and who wants to be with someone nasty?

No matter what your problems or what your fears, you have to smile and pretend nothing's wrong. It makes it easier. We all have difficulties in life from time to time and we shouldn't share it with other people, as they have there own problems.

So much depends on what is in your head

I really consider I have been blessed with my four children

and seven grandchildren. I know that this is the greatest thing in my life now. My business is like one of my children, the school is 54 years old and was born before my children. I love the school, as it involves me with people of all ages. I am working with young people all the time, so that is wonderful. I have to be attuned to them and not be old-fashioned. I get to be a part of their lives. This has gone on for three generations and now with my children, I have the fourth generation – my grandchildren. I love my involvement with my grandchildren.

I went to lunch last week with some St Vincent nuns, and the one who sat next to me was 90. I said to her, 'If I could be like you at 90, I would choose to be 90'. And I would want to be like her, and my aunty who died at 94 and looked 60! If I could be like that, I would live to my 90s otherwise I wouldn't. I would like to live as long as possible, to see my children grow up, who they marry, and be a great-grandmother. I think that would be sensational. I think I'm so blessed to have had children and grandchildren. It is just wonderful. It gives good balance to my life from business. Weekends I can be with them and see them. They often phone and say, 'I love you Nona.'

I have always had the same very strong values throughout life. I think they came from my mother, who was very strong, with good values. She installed them into me. I think they were installed into her from my very strong and wonderful grandfather. I started the model school when I was 22, when I was very young. Then I married and had my children. At that time it was very unusual for a woman to have children and run her own business.

So much depends on what is in the head. When my mother and I came to Sydney we had nothing at all. My mother encouraged me to be successful. Through my efforts, encouraged and helped by my mother, I managed to achieve and gain a tremendous amount of satisfaction. I love achieving, I love being an achiever and I enjoy the challenge of business. I find that coming to work every day is like a game. It's the game of life and business. I run my business very honestly and very on-the-level, otherwise it would not still be here after 54 years. I never take advantage of anybody. People trust me and rely on me. I have all those students, all those generations, and they're my friends. We care for each other and it gives me a chance to give out a lot of love. I get a lot of love in return. I watch the students with eagerness as they grow, improve and feel better about themselves. It's such a great reward.

Be the best you can be

Be the best you can be, is my slogan. I believe that I should take care of myself. I have always believed that. If I don't take care of myself, I'm not in a position to look after my students and my family.

What has got me through the tough times is my strength of character and the need to survive and to succeed. I also pray, because I'm a Christian, and ask the Lord for guidance, and to show me the right way.

I get through all the obstacles with my mental attitude. If I don't have the right mental attitude, then I can't help myself physically. I believe that the mental attitude should come first – what goes on in your head. You can't take care of your body and hope that your brain will function all right. To stay in tune with my body, I talk to my body. I know what my body feels. I talk to my brain and I talk to my soul, and am I'm vitally aware of every part of me.

It worries me the way some things are moving along. Somebody was saying, 'Forget about spelling, you've got spell check. Forget about writing personal letters, you've got your computer.' I think that's wrong, because if you let technology take over then you are going to slip backwards. The human race will slip backwards. Yes, you have to keep yourself up with technology, but I'm a great believer that you must make sure you are well-educated. You can't leave it for the computer to do it for you; you can't leave it to spell check. You have to be able to have good handwriting, so you can sit down and write a nice letter. It may sound old-fashioned but it keeps your brain sharp. You just can't sit there and put your mind into neutral and press buttons.

I don't use a computer, all my staff have computers. In fact I have 20 in the business college. I don't want to spend my time sitting in front of a computer. If I want to look something up on the web, I ask my staff – Lindsay or Jamelie. It gives me physical and mental time to do something else.

I don't use a mobile. After all the years of running a modelling agency, working all day on the phone, then going home and phoning New York and Paris at night, I learnt to hate telephones. I don't even have a message machine at home. If somebody phones me at home and I'm not there, they will phone back another time or phone my office and leave a message there. I see young people addicted to their mobile. They can't put it down; they can't be away from it. They have to be always sending and receiving text messages.

You have to keep your brain challenged and you have to have all this information. I can't use a keyboard but I don't need to. I've got people to do it for me. I write letters. I've written about six or eight letters today, by hand. They are 'thank you' letters. People who receive them will be surprised that it isn't an email, it isn't a fax. It is somebody who cared to sit down and write a personal letter. I think they will appreciate it. My grandfather always made sure I would write well. He said, 'June, you will be judged by your handwriting, do it well.' You have to move with technology, but don't lose the old-fashioned values.

You can't maintain friends unless you go out of your way to keep in touch

I value my good health, my children, my grandchildren and my business. I value my good, good friends who I have had for such a long time. I believe in keeping in touch with them. You can't maintain friends unless you go out of your way to keep in touch, and I do that.

The only thing I regret is all the houses I bought and sold. I wish I had kept them. I never knew that you don't sell your house to buy a new one. Instead, you use that to borrow for your next one and put someone in it to rent it. There are lots of things in business I wish I had known about, instead of finding out now. I really grew up in business just doing it. I teach young men and women all about business and all the things I didn't know when I started.

When we first came to Sydney my mother said, 'You have to go to Business College.' I thought it would be boring and dull, and I would hate it, so I went to be a model. I wish I had done a business course as well as modelling, because it would have been very beneficial during the early years. I made mistakes in business and found out the hard way, but that was why I started the business finishing college. I show them how to make themselves look great, speak beautifully, present well, and have good manners, as well as all aspects of business. I think everyone should go to a business college. I would like them to leave school in year 11 and come to one year in a business college instead of wasting time doing their high school certificate.

Prevention is better than cure
I don't expect to live to any particular age. I would like to live into my 80s. I think that 80 is the crucial age when there is a risk of getting an illness, something to take us away.

I'm very aware of my health. If I think I have a problem, I immediately go to the doctor and get it checked out. I believe that prevention is better than cure, or to get something early at the first signs is very important. I would not want to live far into my 80s unless I was physically and mentally well. I don't want to be a burden. When I speak to my friends, we all feel the same way. We don't want to be a burden to our families, either physically or mentally.

I would like to live as long as I am fit and well, can be

independent, live in my own apartment and take care of myself. Otherwise, please Lord send somebody, send something that takes me away before I'm a burden to my family.

In the next ten years or so, thank the Lord, I want to do what I'm doing now. I love to travel. I want to keep my staff organised so I can travel. I want to keep working hard, being involved and then find time to go and visit my family in Italy and my family in Perth. I'm beginning to ease up a little bit and I have just the greatest staff. I'm going to start coming in a little later and make my days a little shorter.

I think you are as old as you think you feel, so I'm 25. I feel 25, and I intend to stay 25 forever. I don't feel any different to the person I was when I was 25. That was my best year, the most wonderful year of my life. I think when somebody feels old, and some people feel old at 50 or 60, it's all in the mind. I think if you feel old, that's when you become old.

Chapter 8

Owen Denmeade

Owen Denmeade was born in Woolloomooloo, Sydney, and grew up in Bondi. He played fullback for Eastern Suburbs (Rugby League) in 1956. Owen was Head of training at 3M and founder member of the Australian Institute of Training and Development. After 24 years with 3M, he went into advertising, joining Ogilvy & Mather and then George Pattersons, retiring at 61. With an extensive background in sales, marketing and management, he was a regular writer for 'Australian Small Business & Investing' and had his own consultancy 'The Training Works'.

A thoroughly well known Sydney character, both in sporting and advertising circles, Owen has pursued a passion for collecting things. On a Saturday morning you will see him riding at Centennial Park in Sydney, on one of his collection of Malvern Star bikes over 60 years old. Owen also has a passion for golf with his collection of hickory-shafted clubs dating back to the 1920's. He has been happily married to Chloe for over 40 years, with three children and three grandchildren.

Owen has run the City to Surf four times in under 60 minutes and at 64 decided to learn to dance hip hop and funk!

I try to walk, run, swim or ride most days but it's all pretty minor stuff compared to some people. Energy is a comparative thing. You think, 'My god, compared with some people, my energy and activity levels are slack!' Like people who come from 100km bike rides, my energy level compared to them is just ordinary. But then, compared to the guy next door who doesn't do anything!...

Dance, movement, I love it. After years of talking about it, at the age of 64 I eventually went to a course of dance classes, hip hop, funk, cardio. It was so good. The movement and use of isolation was a bit weird, but there was really good music. The big thing was the isolation. She would say, 'Stop moving your head,' and I said, 'I'm not moving my head.' She said, 'You are, and you're moving your knees.' That's the key, being able to move parts of your body on their own. Most of the people there were dance party people, young people who wanted to get some new moves, and it was fun. I loved it and would like to do it again. Apart from all the good music you get to learn all these terms like – Get on down! Wicked!

I don't have a typical day, I only have a recreational day since I retired at age 61, probably too early. My wife gets up at 5.40 every morning to go for a walk, so when the alarm goes off I wake up too and have breakfast by 7:25, usually a light cereal with milk.

I drink too much coffee. Four mornings a week I don't have anything for breakfast: I meet with people, and just have two mugs of cappuccino. I'm not really good on water and only drink about one litre a day.

I'm not madly 'into' diet. For lunch every day since I retired in 1997, I have the same lunch. Six crackers with vegemite, three Vitawheat with cheese and two Sayo crackers with peanut butter and a slice of tomato on top. All that washed down with pub squash.

For snacks, I buy mixed nuts and keep them in a zip plastic bag, and I buy bananas. I love bananas. If I go out on my mountain bike I put two oranges in the bottle container and at some point I'll sit under a tree and eat oranges. I like oranges, I like nuts, and I like bananas, but I'm not having nuts because they've got some health value. I'm just not into diet.

My wife is totally organic and a really good cook and we have just the one meal, dinner at night, which is really nice. We have lots of organic foods, lots of pasta, lots of fish and we have a glass of wine with dinner every night. One night a week we have takeaway, fish or pizza and then on Sunday night we sit and watch our one hour of television a week, with eggs on toast and a good bottle of Chardonnay.

I have dessert every night, my wife will buy organic fruit mince tarts and we go through a stack of ice cream. Sometimes I'll have it with chopped up banana and chocolate sauce on top.

I don't take any supplements or antioxidants, the only thing I have is Vitamin E cream, for when I get a scratch. About every couple of years, I have to get the occasional skin melanomas zapped. Although I don't use sun block, I always wear a cap in the sun, or a cycling helmet.

I have trained the postman Peter to blow the whistle

I only watch one hour of television a week unless Easts football team are playing, or a cycling event like the Tour de France. I read the business and sports section of the Herald every day, and anything else I can. I also listen to a bit of ABC radio daily, mainly to what people are saying. I like music, love Beethoven, Verdi, and love opera, which I discovered really late in life. If I don't have anything to do, I get bored so I just jump on a mountain bike and ride around.

My attitude to technology is terrible. We haven't got a mobile phone in the house and don't use the Internet. We haven't got email and although I've got an Apple Mac, it's used as a typewriter, and we haven't got a fax. I have trained the postman Peter to blow the whistle and I love it. I go up EVERY MORNING and look in the old fashioned mailbox. People have to send me hard copy through the post!

Don't play the age card

In the group I mix with we try not to play the age card, that is, to say how old you are. When someone says, 'But I'm over 60.' We say, 'Mate, don't play that age card.' The worst thing is when someone says, 'Oh, he's good for his age!' I hate that.

Even though I'm an old football player and a marathon runner I haven't had any major injuries, like a lot of people around me. I think it's mainly because maybe I'm running too quietly. Although I run most days, it sometimes is only 10 to 15 minutes.

I run with doctors, and every year I run on a treadmill and have my heart checked. Every year I get a letter saying, 'Awesome, amazing!' – for your age!!!!!! However, I do take Lipitor, which is a cholesterol lowering drug, as my cholesterol was higher than it should be. It wasn't diet related, it was me. I wasn't eating too much fat and cholesterol, I was producing it. My blood pressure is good, and I give blood as often as I can.

I have no upper body strength, which is really annoying, I know this, because I go down to the park with those exercise stations and they have these instructions on what to do. For a beginner they say to only do five chin-ups and I can't even do that! And I'm not flexible and that's an element of fitness – I can't touch my toes. I'm a member of the gym at the football stadium, and never even go there! I should.

Ageing happens and I'm not trying to be young

In the next ten years I expect to be doing more of the same. I don't worry at all about getting older, I'm just thinking it's always going to be just like this. But losing it mentally would be terrible. Maybe if you didn't know you'd lost it, it wouldn't be so bad. But if you knew you were losing it, like my wife's mother at 94, it's just terrible and she really would like to fall off the perch.

You don't want to last longer than your money

I haven't thought about how long I'll live. My mother was 88, and my father was 73 when he died, but I don't think I'm going to die from what they died of. What I do think about is, I hope that the money doesn't run out. Money is important in that you don't want to last longer than your money, because then your life changes. They're suggesting that most of the people working at the moment aren't going to have enough money to retire. If suddenly you find you've got no money then you've got no choices. You can't buy a new bike, you can't do things, and you can't go anywhere. Money's important in that it leaves you with options.

The meaning of life is to become what you are capable of becoming

Fortunately very early, I discovered the meaning of life, which most other people seem to struggle with. The meaning of life is to become what you are capable of becoming.

Get some seeds from the garden shop, such as seeds from a gum tree or an oak tree. Put them in front of you. Then look at a gum tree or an oak tree. This tiny seed could become that! But it may not. If you walk round to the wharf at Parsley Bay in Sydney, you'll see lots of rocks. You can't even see the soil and... suddenly, there's a tree growing! You think. 'Courageous little thing.' Across the other side the same tree is now 40ft high, and this little one got a bum deal, because it didn't get any soil.

The meaning of life is to become what you are capable of becoming. The disappointment is thinking you could have been somebody. People like to blame other people, and they say they had a bad childhood, it was their mother or whatever, but it's up to them.

We are goal-seeking mechanisms

I have learnt a lot from books, management, sales and marketing books, which were my life for 30 years. Everybody feels better when they're moving towards something. We are goal-seeking mechanisms.

A lot of people blame other people for things that happen to them. I believe anything you get, you've earned. You deserve it. We feel best about ourselves when we're moving towards something, something which we have decided is important for us, something we want to have or do. You feel worst about yourself when you haven't got something to move towards, some personal goal – even a small one.

Inside every one of us is a washerwoman

When I was younger, showing off was important to me, but the big thing in my life has always been the people around me. What I value most now is the people around me and the experiences they have provided – family, friends and especially my grandchildren.

I can still remember the names of the people at school. When I played football, I can still remember the names of the coaches, and when I worked for 3M, the managers I worked with. People make you what you are, it's the people in your life who change and influence you, encourage you. I've been very lucky.

The big thing about me is that I'm a washerwoman. About 25 years ago I was reading an article by the Char of Sufi. He said that, 'What you've got to understand, is that we're all washerwomen.' Even when you're sitting trying to communicate with a brain surgeon, doctor, or barrister, what you've got to remember is that inside they're just washerwomen. The same basic thing that will work on a washerwoman will work on him. Inside every one of us is a washerwoman, and inside me is one.

I wash things, I polish things, I clean things. Bryce Courtenay said to me, 'One of the biggest breakthroughs in my life was when I discovered I couldn't wash something, without making something else dirty.' Later this morning I will wash and polish my car, and then I will wash the cloths, and then I'll have to wash the sink where I've washed the cloth.

Play the glad game

My background is in selling and training, and by nature I think I'm optimistic. After 20 years of telling people who had just joined the company how exciting it is, how lucky they are and what fun it is, you learn to play the glad game. If something goes wrong you say, 'Well geez, it could have been worse!'

Find out what you love to do

My advice to people under 30 is to find out what you love to do. As Peter Drucker would say – find what you're meant to do, what God in his infinite wisdom intended you to do. We used to say that to all the work experience people (2,000 went through George Pattersons while I was there). Do what you love to do and then it won't seem like work. Do what God in his infinite wisdom intended you to do.

George Sheehan, running doctor, fabulous, did a film early on about coping with life on the run. He says structure determines function. You look at someone and see their structure, mesomorphic, endomorphic etc and you say, 'You're never going to be a marathon runner but you could be a sprinter.' When you look at someone you can see from his or her structure what they're meant to be physically. But inside, find what you love to do, and then...if you can get someone to pay you to do that...you're laughing! Someone wrote a really good book called, 'Thank God it's Monday', which meant you couldn't wait to get in to work, to do what you love to do.

Most people want to belong to something, be a part of something, something you're not ashamed of, that also provides you with a sense of personal growth, achievement, recognition, variety and challenge.

Security has got to do with growth

My advice to people in their 40s, is to keep looking. You should have sat down and thought, 'With a few changes this could work out OK.' Make changes if you want to. By 40 to 45, you should be a bit happy with yourself. You should feel like you've made some of the right decisions. You should have decided how it's all going to be. 'If I keep doing this, it's not going to end well. I'm going to have to find new tactics, which will give me the sort of life that I want.' Keep making the little decisions with your head and the big decisions with your heart.

The problem is that a lot of people are scared and it's

often to do with security. Most people have no concept of security. We keep talking about a good safe job – not possible! No good job can be safe, no safe job can be good. If it's a good job, it's a challenge, a chance to perform, so it's not safe. Again according to Peter Drucker, the real security is to be a growing person, in a growing organisation, if you're into organisations. A lot of people want to be individuals, but security has got to do with personal growth, not just money.

Motivational theorist Maslow had the concept of self-actualisation. To begin, you need to be warm, you need to have clothing, you need to have food and water, and then you need to belong. After that you think, 'Not only do I belong, but I'm important here.' You go into this weird zone where you're not dependant on anyone. You think, 'Yes, I have become what I am capable of becoming.' Self-actualisation is pretty rare. You think, 'I don't need anyone to tell me how good I am, mate. I know it. I feel that I am what I'm meant to be.'

Old age is when you can't do some of the things you want to do

Old age is when you can't do some of the things you want to do – if you can't get up in the morning and do things, like being able to get on a bike and ride, or kick a football, then you're old. It's about doing things, it's not about having things.

I've got three grandchildren, twin boys, 13, and a boy 3. I reckon I've got to be able to run, jump, bowl, catch, and play football for another 12 more years. You think that impresses them, but it doesn't. We were playing touch football recently and my son said to one of the boys, 'Do you realise that your grandfather is 66,' thinking that he would be impressed, but he said, 'That's disgusting!'

I don't do stress. I get on a bicycle, when you're riding up the hill you're not thinking about anything else but the top of the hill. It erases anything else, like whether you've paid the electricity bill. I don't do stress. I don't do envy. I don't do regret. Sometimes I lie on the floor, or the bed, for hours. In my family it's called, 'He's thinking'.

I'm not a big planner, but I love having projects. When I first retired I used to go to court a lot, it was fascinating. Now I'm thinking I would like to go to meetings of the Institute of Human Resources...these people need help.

You cannot be serious!

John McEnroe was right...when he said, 'You cannot be serious!' You can't be serious. Surround yourself with interesting people who can put up with you and...do what you love to do.

There is a great message from 'The Power of One' when a railway guard on the train says to the little boy PK, 'First with the head, then with the heart, that's how a man stays ahead from the start.' That... is the actual power of one. Think about something until you feel strongly about it, and then go with the heart.

Chapter 9

Roger Climpson

Born in Peterborough, England in 1931, Roger always had one ambition in life, to be an actor. At the age of 20 he won a scholarship to the Royal College of Dramatic Arts in London and left there to be a Shakespearean actor for a while in the West End. In 1952 he came to Australia to do radio drama and was in numerous serials of the day – 'Life Can be Beautiful,' 'When a Girl Marries,' 'Tarzan,' etc. With the advent of television he got a job with TV Channel 9 as a general announcer, reading news, doing documentaries etc.

After nine years, Roger left and did two years free-lance acting, commercials and documentary films. He then joined Channel 7 and became their main newsreader for many years. Roger also compered over 200 episodes of one of Australia's most popular programs 'This is Your Life'. He retired again to make documentaries and to run his father's business after he had died.

In 1989 Roger came back to television to read news again, and his show became the top rated news program in Sydney. Roger was a newsreader for a total of about 30 years. In 1994 because of cancer he retired again. His experience with cancer led him, in association with the Rotary Club of Lane Cove, to set up the Prostate Cancer Foundation of Australia, which is now a national body.

In 1996 he went back to Channel 7 to present a program called 'Australia's Most Wanted', which was a very successful crime-solving program. Since 1999 Roger has been Chairman of the Board of radio station 103.2 FM, Christian Broadcasting Association and produces programs for the Bible Society, especially 'Celebration of Word and Song', the story of Easter, which is presented in the Sydney Town Hall each year.

Roger has been very happily married for almost 50 years, with three children, and five grandchildren. He has received numerous awards for news reading, an award from the Variety Club of Australia, the 1995 Television Award, the Bible Society Award-'Most Outstanding Contribution to the Use of the Bible,' the Rotary Award for Excellence, and a NSW Police Award for 'Australia's Most Wanted'.

At 69 he taught himself to use a computer just before, he says, he got too old.

On most occasions I get up by about 7.30 and get my wife a cup of tea. For breakfast I always have some Wheatbix with fresh fruit. That's a regular understood thing. By 8.30 or 9 am I'm working downstairs in the office under my house. I work on all sorts of projects until round about one o'clock or so, then have lunch. I very often have one of those TV dinners, which I find enjoyable. If possible I like to have the afternoon clear, to go and do what I want to do. I find that if I do more than four or five hours of work a day it seems to gang up on me and I start getting all tense. But it's great if I have something to look forward to in the afternoon, play a game of golf, hit a few balls, or I used to go for a sail. I've got to have something to look forward to in a relaxing way. When I've had a good afternoon out playing golf, win or lose is beside the point. When I come home, I'm relaxed. It's wonderful.

When I get home, I usually have a couple of scotches while I watch the evening news. The way the news is going you need a couple of scotches these days! In the evening for dinner, I usually have whatever my wife Clare suggests. Sometimes it's a salad, sometimes it's a steak, depending. By 10 o'clock I'm ready for bed.

My philosophy is live for today and enjoy today
I don't really have a standard diet; I come and go a bit. For example, at the moment I've been told fish is a very good idea, so I'm on a bit of a fish diet. If my wife Clare goes

onto a diet, I go onto it with her for a while. If I don't like it, I go back onto the old style. I am not somebody that worries all the time about his health. I think when your number's up, your number's up. I think you can spend all this time worrying about your health and go outside and get hit by a bus.

My philosophy is live for today and enjoy today. If you get into a serious situation, where you're clearly desperately overweight, then you've got to something about it. I find my weight seems to come and go a little bit, depending upon how much exercise I do.

I think that because of my age my powers of concentration are getting less. I believe that my success lies in having a capsule of work, which is surrounded by free time. This is obviously something which you can't do when you're normally at work. You walk into the office and the phone goes for eight hours. I don't have to do that any more. I can say, 'OK I'm going to start at 9 or 10 and work till 1 or 2 and that's it!' Whatever's not been done, I'm going to do tomorrow morning, sort of a free-fall situation. When I can do that I'm fine, but when I'm under pressure, when I find I have extra things to do, and I can't get round to doing the things that I enjoy doing, such as go for a walk, or play golf, then I find I start getting very stressed, very tense. That's when I become short tempered. And that is when I could very easily become divorced!

To me, old is a mental state, not a physical one
For exercise I go for a walk or play golf. I play golf once or twice a week, but if I haven't got time to play golf, I go down to the driving range and spend an hour and a half hitting 200 balls.

I go for a walk about once a week for an hour, hour and a half. I go down to the local park and usually walk around about four times. I swim, but not as often as I should. If it looks even vaguely cold I don't go in the water. I don't think I'm a physically energetic person. I honestly believe that the most important thing is what you do mentally. I believe that the mental thing is what gives you old age.

I don't want to live to be old. I want to live to enjoy life for as many years as I can without becoming old. To me, old is a mental state, not a physical one.

I've never really worked, my hobby has always been my job
Why is it that some people at 40 look as if they're 70? I think it's because they've lost track of it all. I think I've been extremely fortunate, very fortunate, because my hobby has always been my job. Therefore I've never really worked in the true sense. My whole love has been what I do, television, acting, presenting, writing documentaries have always been my life, so I've never really worked.

I've never been in the position where I can say, 'I hate this job.' I've never had to do that. I'm not saying I don't get stressed. Yes, you can get stressed because you're doing too much of it, too much of a good thing. But at the same time I've never really been in a situation where I've dreaded the fact that I've got to go to work. I think that is what kills you. I think most people in the world are like that, constantly doing something which they don't really want to do.

There are very few people that fortunately find the sort of job which is not a job but a passion – a way of life which is passionate. Artists often do, but how many people involved in the arts can spend their whole life doing it? Often so many of them have to leave it for a time for one reason or another, usually the fact there's no more work coming.

I've been so fortunate, because at all times I've always been able to continue in this job. Only once did I have to do something else. We had two children, with another one coming and the bottom fell out of the radio acting industry. I had to earn a living, so for several months I became a real estate agent. I hated it! I would go to work thinking, 'Why do I have to do this?' I would make up any excuse to go later or not to go at all.

I believe mental stimulus is the most important thing of all.
In the next 20 years, I see myself continuing to be involved with the radio station 103.2. It's a tremendous challenge to watch it grow and to be part of it growing. That will stimulate me for a while. If I find I am not stimulated, I will write a book. I've already written one book, and there's about four or five books I've been going to write one day. I haven't written them already, because I'm lazy. I tell myself I can't do it now, because I'm too busy. That's rubbish – if I wanted to, I could.

Of course I can put aside a few hours a day to write. The other challenge is that I know that once I do that, I'll give too much time to it. My only experience, having written one book, is the fact that I would come into my office at 9 o'clock in the morning and would keep going until 8 o'clock at night. Then I would go to bed and drive my wife mad, because all I talked about was the book! That's another way in which you can drive yourself crazy.

When I do this next time, can I keep this under control without losing the muse at the same time? I tell myself, maybe I'm putting off the evil hour – most writers put it off and put it off, and then when they start, they can't stop. It's like an alcoholic going back to have a drink. The trouble is that once you start thinking, your mind takes over. 'What about this? What about that? I could do this,' and start waking up in the middle of the night, which is not a good thing. One day I will write another book.

The first book I wrote was about a Downs Syndrome child and that went very well. Even though it was released 15 years ago now, it's still doing very well. I want to do a couple of historical novels and also another one on my son-in-law's father, the most amazing man, a Polish man. His story is unbelievable, and how he came to Australia during the Second World War. An amazing man, I've definitely got a book in mind to do on him.

One of my ambitions has always been to go and write a book on a certain place, then go and live there while I'm writing it.

I have this glamourous image in mind. I admire people who have the guts to do it. We all sit there and think, 'O wouldn't it be great to do this, yeah, yeah, there's this problem and that problem, better forget it.'

When you've got nothing to do, that's when you start to rust
The only time I feel I'm getting old, is when on those rare occasions I've got nothing to do. Then I'm in trouble. I think when you've got nothing to do, that's when you start to rust. It's exactly the same as with a yacht or a car – if you don't use them, they rust and they fall to pieces. You must use it all the time.

I hope to get move involved with golf and spend more time on the golf course. I was a yachtsman for many, many years. The cost was getting so incredibly expensive, so I have given that away, and strangely enough I don't even miss it now. I've taken up golf. I'm a very bad golfer and that is the challenge. I am determined I am going to one day get this right. I'm going to nail it! Golf is a never-ending source of energy and involvement from a physical sense.

It's amazing how many older people play golf. Some of the guys I play with are in their early 80s and they hit an incredible golf ball still. They have found it's become a way of life. I think that's very limiting. I think when you go to that extent, it's a pity if your whole life has to be dedicated just to playing golf. But it does seem to fill in the gaps more and more as time goes on.

You have to live with yourself
I must admit that one of the great problems I find is constantly motivating myself to start each day. That seems to become more difficult as I get older. To actually come down into the office, switch on the computer and do the first job. That I find becomes more and more difficult – I think, 'I might just get another cup of coffee before I start, or I wonder if I should ring up someone? I wonder if Jo's going to play golf tomorrow.' Stop it, get down and do the job! Think about

that when you've finished, not before you start.

The funny thing is that once I start, I become totally involved in it. 'Good heavens, it's half past one already!' I know I've got to come down to the office and get on with the job, because if I don't I will sit upstairs and put on the mid-morning news and sit and watch it! But at the same time as I'm sitting watching it, I will feel totally guilty. Without realising it, I become more and more tense because I'm sitting there subconsciously thinking 'I shouldn't be doing this.'

You have to live with yourself. You have to accept the fact that the most important thing is to come to terms with yourself. I think that as you get older, you have to do it more often. I do it every day, sometimes twice a day – say to myself things like, 'Goodness me, 73 wow, I can't really do much work any more. What would happen, if I hadn't got any money?' For goodness sakes stop all that rubbish, cut it out, you can't think about that. You've just got to think about the next thing that you're going to do. That is negative, negative thinking. Negative thinking is very bad for you. We all do it.

As you get older, all the wrinkles of the past go away

I do think about the past and as you get older, you do think about it more. There are so many things to reflect upon, whether it happened 3 years ago or 20 years ago. The strange thing is that I am beginning to understand that the older you get, the more you seem to reflect further back. Possibly because that's covered with a more rosy hue, I don't know. Probably as you get older, all the wrinkles of that particular time go away and you just see the beauty of it.

You don't see the pain; you just see the glory of the result, forgetting the hell that you went through to get that result. 'Wow, do you remember when we did such and such? Wasn't it incredible when we got ten curtain calls, wasn't that incredible!' You forget the fact that you nearly went mad trying to learn the lines, and you couldn't stand the director, and most of the actors you couldn't get on with!

You forget all that, you just think about what an incredible experience it was, standing on that stage with the curtain calls going up and down. You remember the good things. I'm sure it must be the same when a woman has a baby and goes through absolute agony, and yet within an hour that's all forgotten totally.

Why worry about things that you cannot change
I think as a young man I would have stayed in England longer and I would have stuck with being a Shakespearean actor. I would have tried harder to become an actor, because if I have one regret, that has still been my greatest love. Economically I had to do other things as there wasn't money to be made in Australia as a stage actor, so I gravitated to where the cash was. OK, it was an enormous success, but at the same time I think, 'What would have happened if I had stayed back in England?'
Maybe all the things I dreamed about achieving, such as being a leading stage actor in England, I would have achieved. I've never regretted living in Australia, but the point is if you start being negative about your past that defeats the object too, because you can't change it. Why worry about things that you cannot change? You should be able to say, 'Gee I've had a fantastic life and I've enjoyed it.' I believe that if you think, 'I've had a rotten life,' you are thinking negatively and you start destroying yourself.

Youth is a gift, age is an art
I would ask someone in their 20s to listen to people that are older than they are. Listen to the philosophies of the older people. Stop saying, 'Oh I know it all'. Stop thinking, 'I am going to be like this forever.' It's rubbish because eventually you're going to be older too. Try to learn early on the secret of old age. There is a saying which goes, 'Youth is a gift. Age is an art.' I think that is absolutely correct.
A young person needs to realise that they will get older. I know that youth doesn't tend to do that, but tends to only

think for the moment; 'I will live forever.' Young people need to think ahead, and not ignore what the older people have to say – not necessarily about how to work a computer, but about life itself, the living of life, every aspect of it. And they need to try to understand that as you get older, you will think differently. If you can be armed with information about that next stage of life as you get to it, I think you'll find it far less bumpy.

Age is not the controlling factor – it is mental approach
My message to someone in their 40s is not to give up hope. When you hit 40 you think, 'Oh, goodness my youth is gone, all I can see is wrinkles, more and more of them growing ever rapidly. What am I going to do? Where's my life going? I haven't achieved anything I wanted to achieve.' Cool it – at 40 you've got a long way to go. A long way to go, don't give up. There are many people who don't make it until they're 50, 55 or even 60. Just keep going, try to achieve what you want to achieve, don't assume that age is the controlling factor for everything. It is not.

Age is not the controlling factor – it is mental approach. It's the state of your mental age, not physical age. Keep going, keep trying. It's amazing. I'm astonished at myself really. I didn't really start getting there until I was about 50!

My view on age is that it's a state of mind, a total state of mind. What you tell your mind is what you are. What you tell your mind about your physical being, is what you are. I believe your physical being is secondary to your mental being. What you are in your mind is all that matters.

How is it that some people can be so crippled and yet do the most amazing things? Look at that man sitting in a wheelchair, who's one of the most brilliant mathematicians in the world. How can he train his brain to do that! Whatever he's done is what is him, not the body sitting in the chair. He is what his brain is doing. Three people sitting in the room and you can pick out the one that's really 'with it' mentally, the one that has got far more get up and go than all the others put together.

I don't want to look like you!
All my life I've been conscious of physical appearance because of being in front of a television camera five nights a week, so I look after my skin and use aloe vera on it every day. I had a facelift done many years ago, and I never regretted it. I wouldn't do it again. Why would I want to? It doesn't matter any more.

I've managed to escape any skin cancer, which is very lucky, seeing as I sailed for many years. Yachting is very hard on your skin, you're in all weathers all the time, but I always put block-out on and it seems to have put me in very good stead. Out on the golf course, the guys say, 'Why the dickens are you putting that on?' and I say, 'Because I don't want to look like you!!!'

What is to be will be
I've had three major things that were earth – shattering at the time. In 1946, I had to have a left lapectomy in my lung from playing rugby. A rib went into my lung and damaged it, and they took a piece of my lung away. Around 1961 I had very serious hepatitis, they thought it was cancer of the liver. It wasn't, and I got over that. In 1994 I had a radical prostectomy for cancer, very fortunate they got it at the right time and they got the whole lot.

The first two, I knew in theory I should get better. The lung – I was only 15 or 16 at the time. I was still a kid and just assumed, 'O well, it's going to be fine'. Life was. I got over it no problem. Hepatitis yes, I thought that got a bit worrying, but I thought I would get better and I did. But the cancer one is very different. You're not sure that you are going to get better.

Prostate cancer is one of the least understood forms of cancer that there is. It affects as many men per year as breast cancer affects women, but the ladies have done far more about it. They're formed organisations and committees.

They've got government support. They do something about it. They will stand up and be counted. The men don't want to know about it. Somehow it's an area they don't even want to talk about. It's a personal thing; they just don't want to know. Even if they get it, or have a problem with it, they feel there's some sort of shame in having a problem there, and they won't talk.

When you get prostate cancer, you frankly don't know where you stand, because there are many things you can do. You can have an operation, you can take drugs, etc and the specialist does not tell you which one you should do. He says, 'Those are the options, you decide.' Now that means you've got to make the decision, you've got to decide which lottery you're going to enter, and just hope you pick out the winning ticket as well. And that is the problem with prostate cancer. You have the operation and after you've done it, you still don't know if you made the right choice. It takes a long time afterwards before you know. I was very fortunate, I chose the operation and it was a 100% success.

I think this has given me the philosophy that what is to be will be. I think if you think positively, many of things may not even come to fruition. I think the body can heal itself with the power of the mind. I've got no clinical backup for the statement, but I believe that very strongly.

The big secret is to have three good meals a day
I have low fat foods, like low fat ice cream, and not a lot of fried food, my wife protects me from that. As far as I'm concerned bacon and eggs would be my favourite food, so I'm not allowed to have it very often, until I start moaning and bacon and eggs turns up. I don't really consciously make an enormous effort in relation to diet. I know I'm probably wrong, and I know I should feel guilty, but I don't.

Sometimes I'll have a little jam tart, but I have to be very careful, because I'll probably end up having two or three. I could become addicted very quickly to sugar and sweet things, but I've reduced that a lot over the last few years.

I don't constantly think to myself, 'O goodness can I eat that?' If I want to eat it, I eat it. But I try to be sensible about how much I have, and how often. I don't consciously say, 'Because I had that I mustn't have this.' To me that's a form of agony.

I don't like junk food. With due respect, I don't like MacDonald's. People fill themselves up with quick food and it has a detrimental effect on their health in the long term. I think the big secret is to have three good meals a day. We occasionally have pizza. I sometimes, every two or three weeks, have fried fish and chips which I love, but I can see that it can't be good for you. While consciously I don't say, 'I'm not going to eat it', I subconsciously think, 'We won't have it too often.'

I don't want to have to worry about my physical self

I have had a weight problem. I don't believe in cholesterol and all that rubbish. I don't want to know about it. I don't want to have to worry about my physical self. My weight comes and goes a bit – it gets worse when I'm stuck in the office and start eating all the wrong stuff.

I'm not your average person, in terms of being concerned about what I should do physically with myself. I know I'm the exception, I know I should be caned over the hand for it, but that's the way I am. I get my blood pressure checked every three months or so, and every year blood tests to check my cancer – everything's all right. It's fine. There's a friend of mine who worries himself silly all the time about his physical health. He's always at the doctors, 'Why have I got this and why that?' I can see this guy gradually crumbling up, because he spends his whole life internalising about his physical self.

I was, for a while, taking vitamins. I've stopped taking them because it doesn't seem to make any difference. I was always concerned about colds. Colds were the biggest problem I had as a newsreader. And as a freelance actor or commercial voice, they cancel all your work if your voice is not up to scratch.

I started taking the supplements when I was about to leave channel 7, and amazingly all the colds stopped. But then at one stage I went through a phase where I hadn't got any tablets, so I didn't take them. I got out of the habit and I said to myself, 'Hang on a minute, I'm not getting any colds anyway.' So again, how much of it is in the mind? How right are the doctors in the philosophies of modern thinking and modern science? I don't know it all, but I do know a lot of it is up here in the head!

How much of it, is in the mind?

One of the reasons I'd be terrified to do a stage play now is the remembering of the lines. Then again, I think that is a mental condition. I tell myself that I couldn't do it. I've got to somehow un-tell myself – one can do that, if you have to. How often do you have a physical pain in your leg or something that goes on and on and on, and you decide to see the doctor. He says, 'Oh, it's this or it's that, there's virtually nothing you can take for it,' and the next day it's gone. To me, that's again a mental condition. Once I've been told by somebody it's all right, I know it's all right, and I forget it.

I did find for a while there that I was getting certain problems of going to the toilet, constipation which was bad. I found that one of the greatest things to stop that is water, and so I now drink six or seven glasses of water a day. I also find red wine has a drying effect, and I've now adopted the idea that if I have a glass of wine I follow it with a glass of water. I drink alcohol daily, probably three glasses of Scotch and sometimes a glass of wine with the meal too. Again, what are you doing it for if you're going to worry about it and say, 'I shouldn't do it?' I wonder if you put more strain on yourself. Enjoy it. How many years do you intend to live? To me 85 would be as far as I can see.

My mother died at 98, but my father was 67. He died of a massive heart attack; my mother's heart was the heart of a bull, incredibly strong. That's what gave her the length of life. In fact everything else went, and her heart was still going. There's two ways of looking at this; one is that you are physically very strong, and you go mentally, the other is that you are mentally very strong and you go physically. I think the second one is far worse, because I've seen Clare's mother die, where mentally she just quietly drained away and she was no longer with us. But my mother physically disintegrated, until she was in bed with a brain which was as sharp as a 40 year old, and the pressure and the frustration she had with that was incredible. If I have a choice, that is what I would like to happen. I would just like to slow down, rather than the other way.

The thing that does concern me is the fact that people start to regard you as rusted, even before they listen to what you're trying to say. There was a time when society was designed in such a way that every part of society was utilised by the members of that society. I mean in the days of the jungle, the tribe would ensure that the older people would be used to take care of the children and to educate the children, while they went out and did the work of the tribe. The older people were held in enormous esteem, and that way the whole tribe was unified with a purpose.

Listen to older age, Youth is not everything

It's all gone. We now have a situation where youth is everything. Youth is not everything. Sure, youth has the sharper brains, but it does not necessarily know everything. Older age must have some value simply because of experience and experience does not change, experience of life is still the best way of understanding life. I think people should listen to older age. They should give them a chance, and stop saying, 'Because they've got this number of lines on their face, I will listen to this percent!' Don't judge a book by its cover. Open the book and get some information from it, and then decide if the book's any good. Don't just say, 'I don't like the cover.' Just because you can't walk as fast doesn't mean you can't think as well.

I am concerned about the situation of ending up in a nursing home. That is something I find terribly hard to come to terms with in my mind. I think that's degradation. Even the best nursing homes I've visited show it's very, very, hard to have dignity. I hope that in my case – and I'm sure many older people think the same way – I would rather pack it in before I reach that stage. Not that you have the choice, you don't.

I also think it's within your mental power to pull the plug. I've seen that particularly happen with Clare's mother. A few months ago she was living quite comfortably in this little retirement village, and all of a sudden it all went wrong and she fell apart. And one day she had to go from that little room she had which was her home, to a nursing home where she just had a bed with three other ladies. She was there a week. Suddenly she thought, 'That's it!' I think that demonstrates the power of the mind.

This world is a learning process

I'm a very strong Christian. I believe there is a power beyond you that you can rely on. And if you try to set your measuring stick to God, then I believe you will always strive to be better. I accept the fact that there is someone up there who can help me. I find that is the greatest comfort I have. When I had prostate cancer that was the one thing that kept me from going completely round the twist, not knowing if I was ever going to overcome it.

I didn't just have the cancer; when the operation was taking place there were complications, major complications, and nobody knew exactly how to overcome those complications. I had visions of myself being in hospital for six months and then ending up a cripple – I didn't know. That's what kept me sane, my belief in something beyond this. This world is a learning process as far as I'm concerned. It's not the end, it's the beginning of it. What you learn here, you'll take with you to the next place.

The most important thing in this world is love

I have always valued the importance of being honest, to always tell the truth, to always treat people the way you would like them to treat you. Have a conscience – it's important. People who have a conscience have far more worries, but I think they're far more direct. They live a better life. And the most important thing in this world is love, in all its forms. Love. If you can, try to live your life with that philosophy; and also obey the laws of the land, and control the base of emotions which often get out of hand – temper in particular, and rudeness. I think if you constantly try to work on that you'll become a better person. In other words you've got to be able to live with yourself first. If you can't live with yourself you're in big trouble. That's how I try to live with myself.

'If I speak with the tongues of men and of angels and have not love I am nothing.'

Now what I value the most in life is my wife, my youngest grand-daughter, and the Lord Jesus Christ. When I was younger it was myself, my wife, money and the kids.

My goals for the next ten years or so are to become calmer and to have a greater understanding of love. Also, to have a greater ability to live with myself and accept myself for what I am. It's a growing process, it never stops, I don't think.

My major purpose in life is to fulfil this one and to strive to be closer to achieving some sort of quality or ability with Jesus Christ, to try to be more like him. The more I can get like him, the more I've achieved and the greater I will enjoy whatever it is that comes after this. Because if nothing comes after this, what is the point of it all? If this is the end of it, good gracious me!

It's when you've got time to think about yourself that you have trouble

I like to have a challenge. Two things challenge me and keep me very busy. One is producing, with 250 performers, the Story of Easter for the Bible Society, which I do each year at the Sydney Town Hall which is broadcast by satellite around the world. The other challenge is the Christian radio station 103.2. Over the last three years we've gone from a little station that no one had heard of, to premises at Seven Hills that 2WS used to have. We're probably without question the biggest community radio station in Sydney. We're growing in size and power, and that's a tremendous undertaking, it's really starting to go places. We've got something like 150,000 -200,000 people a week listening to us, which is big for a little community station.

I am constantly stimulated mentally by being involved with the day-to-day requirements of running the radio station. The challenges they throw at you; 'What should we do about this? There's a board meeting, how are we going to fix this problem? We're lacking in cash for some reason, what do we do?' You haven't got time to think about whether your back hurts slightly, or whether you find you're limping for some inexplicable reason. You forget it, it goes away, and you forget it all. It's when you've got time to think about yourself that you have trouble.

I've thought about getting back into theatre; if the right part came along I could probably have my arm twisted. But I think the trouble is that I've spent so much of my time out of the theatre, so much in television, that people have forgotten that I was first and foremost an actor. I've become a TV personality, whatever that means. They expect me to always be myself, but I'd love to have a character part, I'd love that.

Every person is a human being with the same basic problems as every other human being
Several people have inspired me during my life. Lord Louis Mountbatten was one – he was one of the greatest men that walked the earth, in my time. What he did, how he did it, the power he had and the way that he used it; he was a great, great man. I know that Prince Charles has always held him in high regard. If Lord Louis Mountbatten had been alive, I

don't reckon any of the current world situation would have taken place.

Walter Kronkeit was, I think, the greatest English-speaking newsreader the world has ever known. He's a humble man, a lovely, lovely man. I had the pleasure of meeting him – he's a tremendous guy. In addition the other great man who inspired me, and is now dead, was Weary Dunlop. He was a great, great Australian. He was the guy who was the Christ of the Burma railroad in the Second World War, a prisoner of war. Even the Japanese appreciated him so much that they allowed him to move up and down the different camps taking care of the allied prisoners. An amazing, amazing man. I had the pleasure of doing 'This is Your Life' on him.

I was very proud to have the privilege of compering for four years 'This is Your Life', that was absolutely unbelievable. You met so many wonderful, wonderful people from so many different walks of life and you realised that each and every one of them was a human being with the same basic problems as every other human being. They have concerns about the future, their family, their past, their fears, and worries, no matter who they are. But they all have different ways of overcoming life's challenges.

Live your life, and stop worrying about yourself
I haven't got a great deal of time for the constant ongoing theories of doctors, and advances in science. If you did all the things you were asked to do by the doctors and the specialists, you wouldn't have time to live. They all have got some special thing you must do, for this particular problem. I don't accept any of that. What I'm saying is, 'Live your life, get on with your life and stop worrying about yourself. Look out beyond yourself, don't keep looking into yourself.' If you look into yourself, you create more and more rust, because you worry more and more, about less and less.

The people that are incredible are those that get on and do something. They live a life, not like people who say, 'What on earth would happen if I went blind?' Why don't you say, 'If I went blind I would dedicate myself to learning to understand Braille, so that I could continue to do the things I do now.'

That's a positive attitude, which I believe is the most important thing in life. The more you can develop that, the longer you will live and the better you will be, and the more you will enjoy life.

Chapter 10

Dulcie Hume

Dulcie lost her mother when she was only nine and learnt early on the meaning of hard work, working in her father's hairdressing business and looking after the household. Because of the depression her education finished at the age of 14; she went on to make a living as a dressmaker and worked during the war dry-cleaning the uniforms of the American soldiers.

Following on from a passion for swimming, Dulcie started a Royal Life-Saving Club with her first husband and taught over a thousand youngsters. Her sport has kept her going through all the tough times – running, basketball, cycling, dancing, and now walking, aerobics, yoga, and bowls.

She married three times, Arthur, Bill, then Cliff, but as she says, 'I neglected to get a medical clearance on them before marrying them!' She lost all three and then also lost her only son Colin, who died at the age of 47.

At 88 Dulcie, against the advice of her friends, packed up her house and moved with her dog Willy, 400km north to a retirement village. She loves it, is meeting new friends (including a gentleman caller), still does aerobics with the television and her next 'project' is learning to play croquet.

I can still remember when I was a tiny little girl about five, walking into a chemist shop and holding onto Mum's long skirt. I was watching these glass vessels with coloured water and somehow I walked out of the shop holding onto the skirt of another lady, who I thought was Mum. I lost my mother when she was 36. She had a cyst and would not be operated on and it just poisoned her whole system. I was only nine then and it was hard without a mother, but I had a wonderful father, he was great.

We lived in Brisbane, Queensland, and I became a housekeeper at 11 years of age, looking after my brother and my father. Dad was a hairdresser and he had four men working for him, in his men's saloon. They used to wear white coats, which I would wash and iron. I cleaned the saloon and Dad gave me one and six for that, which was a lot of money in those days.

My brother got married, and two months later I met a young man, Arthur, and we were very friendly. He was going to be transferred from Brisbane to Sydney and he asked me to marry him. My brother said, 'You mustn't leave Dad, you can't leave Dad' and I said, 'But you got married didn't you!' Dad said, 'Of course you're going, it's your life.' My brother hardly ever spoke to me again. I was 22 when Arthur and I got married and came to live in Sydney for three years. We had a wonderful time and spent all our wages.

I would work doing any little job, sewing mostly, helping dressmakers. Sydney is such a wonderful place to spend money and have such a good time. In those days we only had a bicycle each, but we used to pedal all the way from Avondale, on one side of Sydney, right over to the beach at Brighton-le-sands. Many a night I was saddle-sore, but we never even thought about cars in those days, and we couldn't afford them anyway.

My husband worked as a commercial discounter, or moneylender, and was studying to be an accountant. Everything changed when the war broke out in 1940 and we were transferred to Melbourne. My husband was in the forces and he had a wonderful captain, but fortunately he wasn't allowed to go overseas because his eyesight wasn't good enough. Arthur actually died with a brain tumour and one of the symptoms was poor eyesight, but no one knew at the time. Anyway, we had a pretty good time in Melbourne. We went to all the dances and I went to work at a huge drycleaners there. There were about 400 employees, and I always said I enjoyed it so much that we should have paid the owners to work there! It was wonderful.

We had the contract for the American soldiers at the time. They would send their uniforms down by the ton. It was a huge business and they were so fussy with their pressing. I was the spotter, who took out stains and looked after the material of the garment. It was very interesting. We had lovely frocks coming in as well as the uniforms, and they were treated so differently to what they are now. In those days the frocks were crepe material, which couldn't be washed and we had to dry-clean them. It's marvellous how fashion has changed.

I was not educated during the depression. I wanted to go to high school, but we were lucky to survive with my Dad's work during the depression. People couldn't afford to go to the barbers and started cutting their own hair and that's when safety razors came in. There was no money coming in and my Dad said he couldn't afford to send me to high school. I was about 14, I cried. It was the end of education for me. But there was always tennis, swimming and the bikes. I did everything, basketball, running and cycling, but swimming was my favourite. I just love to be in sport, and that's how I grew up and was able to cope with all the work I had to do.

When the war ended, we came back to Queensland to live. We thought about having a family and I was getting onto 33. I had to have lots of treatments and so did hubby, but we eventually got going and I became pregnant. We had a son, Colin, who was a big delight. He was a lovely, big baby. He grew 6'3" tall and was very intelligent. He went to high school and then onto university and did very well. He was doing electrical engineering, but he wanted to travel so he gave that all away and started travelling.

Colin was about 18 or 19 when his father died, and I married again about 12 months later. I think if you have had a good marriage you encourage yourself to marry again, to have the experience again. I met Bill over in Chicago, visiting friends, and we came back to settle in Australia. We had a very happy life together. We used to stop at motels and Bill would play on the piano – he was very gifted and a wonderful man. My second husband and I had 15 years together.

My son's marriage broke up and he was very down. He neglected his study and started drinking. He gave me the impression he didn't want to live. He was only 47 when his kidneys eventually went on him, and he died. That was about five years ago.

I lost my second husband and got married again to Cliff. He was a lovely dancer and a good sportsman. We got on so well together but unfortunately we only had six wonderful years together because he was a heavy smoker and got emphysema. I was a zombie for some time after that, but then my body got revived and up I went again. There was another man in Holbrook who asked me to marry him, but I never answered.

I have always been into sport. My first hubby left me quite well off and I didn't have to work, but I did lots of charity work plus sport, swimming and dancing. He and I started a surf life-saving club and we taught over a thousand youngsters marching, and entered the surf carnivals. I still do aerobics with the TV at half past six and so does my dog Willy. Unfortunately these days I miss my swimming, after all those years. I didn't smoke myself, although a lot of my friends did in my young days. You can't swim and smoke. I do plenty of walking; Willy and I walk every day for about three quarters of an hour, sometimes we do two or three walks. I also played indoor bowls last year.

I'm very fussy with my food. I had grilled fish for breakfast today, but I mostly have Weetbix or cooked oats with fresh orange juice on them. I use a lot of skim milk and no sugar, of course. Some mornings for a change I'll have dates and prunes which I have soaked the night before.

I drink mostly hot water, and some mornings I will have a cup of tea. I don't drink tea near a meal and I don't drink coffee at all. For lunch I have grilled steak or chops and plenty of vegetables – no butter and not a lot of salt. Sometimes, I like a cup of tea in between meals, but nothing to eat. I don't buy biscuits or cake. Sometimes when I go to one of those big shopping centres, I go to Wendy's and have a soft ice cream. That's a real treat.

I don't eat late at night. I find as I get older I digest my food better at mid-day. I hardly eat anything at night time just a sandwich or a piece of wholemeal toast. I eat lots of fruit and veggies and a little bit of the canola or olive oil margarine. I drink lots of water and hot water. I also like a beer too, only one a day and I think that has kept me going. I don't ever drink the light stuff just the normal beer. I often have a glass of low fat milk with my meals, especially at lunchtime. Occasionally I'll have a very little bit of wine when I go to a function – it's a real treat.

I have one little tablet a day for my inactive thyroid, and I take two little blue tablets for liquid around the heart. I did have a bit of bladder trouble when they did the hysterectomy, six or seven years ago, but I got over that. 40 years ago I also had an operation for carpel tunnel syndrome in the hands. It was all through sport; sometimes we do a lot of damage through sport. I've had a knee replacement for one knee where the cartilage was worn and the bones were rubbing together. I came through really well because I was swimming, and I've never had any more trouble with it.

I think it's important to eat sensibly and have good thinking. Some people think badly. It's important to keep yourself happy, and have something to look forward to. I thought about this little retirement village for years. When I told my friends at 88 that I was moving, they were horrified; 'You're too old to shift,' they said. I said, 'Maybe I am, but I'm going to give it a go.' And I did.

Don't worry till worry comes
One of my main sayings is, don't worry till worry comes. Some people worry all the time. You don't need to worry all the time. You want to think bright and happy. Why worry till worry comes?

I think you always have to have a project. At the moment I have a very simple project – I was thinking about joining the croquet club. It looks a hard game and that's a challenge. You must have a challenge, it urges you on and keeps you going.

I first went to a yoga class in Melbourne with this stepdaughter of mine and loved it. I thought it was wonderful and I kept going to the class for a long time. We went on a voyage to England and I got asked to help with the teaching of yoga on the ship. I started and 70 people came the first day and 100 came the next day. They gave me the ballroom because the class was so big, and I taught yoga till we got to London. I still do the deep breathing and quite a few of the exercises.

I meditate quite often, depending on whether I need it. Especially when I first go to bed, I love to relax and meditate. I can relax anywhere. I can even sit in a chair and relax.

I read a lot – true stories. I can't stand fiction. But it's getting a bit hard at my age, because you get very tired and concentration runs out of steam. I only watch news on television and like to read the newspapers. I'm very fond of jazz music and good food. I'm sleeping well and enjoying life. I feel well, so what more do I want? I've got everything.

I leave all hurdles I have jumped over behind
I don't sit thinking about the past, I look forward to tomorrow. I leave all hurdles I have jumped over behind. What's the use of going over and over it? I never live in the past. I think of the past as something wonderful. All those ups and downs, they were sent to me to challenge me and I got over them. I think about what I going to do tomorrow. When I wake up in the morning, I plan my day and I'm always ready in plenty of time to go out.

I'm not a bit technical, I feel as though that is just a bit beyond me. I don't feel I want to go any further with technical stuff. At my age I just want to relax, and I'm happy with what I have.

I do have a bit of skin trouble. I have had a lot of small operations for skin cancers. Living in Queensland, it's the worst place for skin cancer. I think I neglected my skin, and also working in the dry cleaners we couldn't get the proper gloves and used to have spirit on our hands which dried them up. Fortunately I used to always wear a hat on the beach and I think that saved my face.

I don't worry or think about the next ten years, really. If I'm lucky I will make it, and if I don't, I don't. I just want to live in this little place in the retirement village. It's something I wanted and I love the people -they're so friendly and nice.

My advice to younger people is – don't be too impulsive. You have got to steady down a lot, and learn yoga. I often see young people who should be doing yoga; they're so tense and not a bit relaxed. Stress can lead to so much bad health in your body.

Middle age was 60, now its 70 because there are so many living to the age of 80, now we probably eat better and do more exercise. Try to get the natural food, instead of all those pills, and walking is marvellous. Keep active and don't slow down. You can't just sit in a chair and do nothing. Keep active; it makes you feel so good. Get plenty of fresh air and deep breathing is so important, it gives you more oxygen.

I never worry about getting older. My first husband used to say, 'I never want to get old,' and he got his wish by dying at 58, but I never think on those lines at all. It never worries me because I don't feel old. I don't feel 88, I feel more like in my 60s.

It's important not to lose your sense of humour
It's important never to lose your sense of humour. You have to think right and hold your head up and keep exercising. Exercise is so good when you experience trouble, and it gives you such a lift.

My father had a great sense of humour and I learnt a lot from him. Some people are dreary, but I try to look for fun wherever I go, whatever I do. I think bright and think it's important not to be serious – I never am. I am having a good innings for which I am very grateful. I am enjoying my later life, and every day is a bonus.

Keep well and don't forget the importance of challenge in your life, never lose that. Always have a project, all your life. That's what I feel. Once you lose that idea, I think you have had it.

Chapter 11

Bob Rogers

Bob Rogers was born on a soldier's settler's farm in Donald, Victoria in 1926. In 1940 his family moved to Melbourne and he got his first radio job in 1942. Bob then went to Tasmania, became one of Australia's first disc jockeys, and at the age of 22 he married his wife Jerri.

Bob moved to Brisbane and by 1958 had over 20 sponsored programmes. He then moved to Sydney to do the top 40 for 2UE. In 1964 Bob was chosen to represent his network on the legendary tour by the Beatles through Europe, Asia, and Australia, where Bob became known as 'the fifth Beatle'.

Bob went into television with The Bob Rogers Show which ran for five years on the Channel 7 Network. Then, after starting a chain of Women's dress shops in 1982, Bob returned to radio and today at 79 still hosts the morning show on 2CH – Monday to Friday, and also the Saturday Night Reminiscing program.

In 2002 John Singleton honoured Bob with a celebration of his 60 years in radio, flying out Chubby Checker especially for the occasion. Bob's current contract runs out at the age of 80, but knowing Bob an extension could be negotiated!

I am an avid newspaper reader, I just love to get up at 6 o'clock and read the newspapers. I've been a media junkie all my adult life. When I went into morning radio I needed to talk about more serious stuff. I couldn't do talk-back because I don't think that talk-back was legal until about 1967, but with the Bob Rogers Program I interviewed every artist that came to town.

I started reading the paper and looking for all sorts of stories and I just became addicted to it. I like to be informed and even though I don't do much in the way of comments these days, I still do love reading the papers.

After my paper I have a light breakfast and get off to work. I have a couple of pieces of toast (I hate cereals), and a boiled egg every second day, and of course a cup of tea. I'm a big tea man, only ever one cup. I go to work about 8, and I'm on the radio from 9 to12. While I'm on the air I have some black coffee, and a little piece of cake, because I gave up sugar years ago. In fact, when my friend Frank was here last week, he has sugar and we couldn't find the sugar! I also don't eat any chocolates. I don't eat as much fruit as I should, just two pieces at work, that's about it.

I'm lucky that at the moment I've always finish work by one o'clock. I probably only work half a day, although there was a lot of preparation in the early days. I come home and prefer to have a sandwich, quite a big lunch. I use Logical and try not to eat too much of it. I eat a lot of bread, I must admit. I have not eaten white bread for years, always brown multigrain, even though it's expensive bread. It's an interesting thing, but in the afternoon I don't need anything.

Power Nap
I do have what's now called a 'power nap'– ten minutes, no more, no less. It's all I need. I sit out in the back garden, usually in the sun, and it's only ever ten minutes. After I wake up I usually go for my hour's walk, every alternate day, and then at 5 o'clock I go to the club and have a couple of beers.

I used to live on a farm, and I swear to you, when I left the farm at 14 the only greens I knew were beans and peas. I'm fascinated that today peas aren't so popular because no one wants to spend the time podding them. But we had to buy things that would last and survive the heat.

It's very interesting; every meal we had potatoes, and I love potatoes still. When my wife goes away, I don't go out for meals, I don't buy ready-made meals. I put a couple of potatoes in the steamer, I always have a green, and nine times out of ten I have fish. I drink a bit of red wine and have an occasional lamb chop, grilled.

My mother was the world's worse cook, so I deserved to have a wife who's a very good cook, When we're having people over my wife will cook as many as five vegetables, but she's an extremist. We also have our own garden, and she does a lovely creamed spinach. When I was a kid, spinach was the last thing in the world you wanted!

I chew a couple of vitamin tablets every night; I've convinced myself I need that, then go to bed about 9.30 and listen to Philip Adams.

Find something you're passionate about

There is a saying in a wonderful book called 'How to Lose Friends and Alienate People', by a fellow called Toby Young. This is very important philosophy of my life, but it's more easily said than done:

'Find something you're passionate about, something you can't not do.'

You'd be surprised how quickly everything falls into place, when you're doing something you really love. Unfortunately, a lot of people never find it.

Life's been very good to me, I'm a worker, a workaholic. I don't want to retire. I've found that friends of mine who have retired, who are younger than I am, have invariably become very old men. Work keeps me alert.

When I was younger I was ambitious, and have been told I spent too much time at work. When we came to Sydney, it was incredibly competitive. I was competing with a fellow called John Laws, so I'd go to all these functions, everywhere. That was part of my personality on air, to be everywhere and know what was going on. I was an old gossip, they loved all the gossip and they listened to me for that.

One secret of my success is a persistent wife

My health is the most important thing to me now; I took it for granted until I got cancer. At the age of 41, I had a heart problem, and it's only through a persistent wife that I survived. I used to wake up in the middle of the night and try and get rid of the bubbles in my ears. She said, 'You might have blood pressure.' So I went to the doctor and told him what my wife said. He said, 'Your wife should be a doctor, you've got blood pressure.' By the third ECG I realised I had hardening of the arteries, so I smartened up my life.

I was overweight, so I took quite a bit of weight off. I cut back my drinking, tidied up my life, lost sufficient weight and within six months I got an A1 report. That was when I started to play tennis, exercise and look after myself.

I thought I'd better take up walking, so I walk down Awaba St (which is very steep) and up Beaconsfield, it's a longer slower hill. Tennis was part of my life for 30 years; I used to go three times a week. I only gave up because of inconvenience; the traffic was so bad that I decided I wasn't going to spend my life in a motorcar. Now I walk an hour every alternate day and I almost always, if I have to go to the shops, walk there – that's about a 10 to 15 min walk each way.

It was no wonder I had the hardening of the arteries, because on the farm you killed the fatted lamb, not the calf. I used to help my Dad get the sheep and we'd kill it, and he'd skin it. That would last us for quite a while. Milk, butter, which you made yourself, and cream, everything was high cholesterol. Very little fruit. The end result is I've been on diuretics for four or five years. I'm on a pill for blood pressure, and something else for high cholesterol. I'm appalled when I see people buying those big cartons of chips, usually with tomato sauce on them. They're delicious to eat but I never touch them any more.

One secret of my success is having a persistent wife. She pushed me into doing something about my heart problem, and then a couple of years ago she forced me into doing something about the lower stomach pains I was having.

I had been back on the air full-time for seven years and had only had two days off, and they'd been for funerals of old friends. I had just turned 74. On 7 December I went on the air and said, 'Tomorrow I won't be here.' I didn't say why, but I was having a colonoscopy, which I should have had years before.

All the boys at tennis used to talk about it, but not me. I had what they called the silver saddle. I drank all that dreadful stuff, went in the next day and got the wrong result; 'You've got cancer.' So I decided to stay in hospital and have the operation the next day. Thank goodness, I got it early.

When the oncologist came into the Mater Hospital to see me, Mike Gibson had just come in with his wife to see me. The doctor interrupted to give his report and say, 'You will have to have chemotherapy.' The first thing a man says is, 'Will I lose my hair?' Before the doctor could answer, Mike says – 'If he does, can I have first refusal?' After that I had six months of chemotherapy, and I still have lots of hair, Mr Lucky, that's me.

That song 'Always look on the bright side of life' is such a good theme. Looking on the bright side of life is not just an admirable quality, I believe it could help you beat cancer. I didn't beat it, but I'm determined to keep it away now.

Doing it tough

I have another serious belief that only came out a few months ago. I think that people today are far too concerned about keeping their children healthy, not letting them eat anything that might be bad for them, and making them drink water out of a bottle etc. They're not giving their young immune systems any chance to build up any strength against nasties. Whereas if you grew up on a farm like I did, without any electricity, this means no refrigeration. I never saw hard butter except in winter; it was always melted because all you had was the safe. Water was always out of a tank, and often the possum or a dead bird had been in the tank, and all you'd do is take him out and drink the water.

I really believe that tough 14 years on the farm has made a difference; my sister's 83, my brother's 80, I'm 77 and my other brother's 74.

My parents had nothing, and neither did Jerri. Jerri wanted an education and I wanted security. I just wanted a good job so I could have the kids looked after. I waited four years for a pushbike. I lived on a farm and went to school on a horse, three of us on a horse. I was about ten when I finally got the pushbike, and I can tell you the colour, the brand, how much it cost and where we bought it. As soon as I got that pushbike, I never rode a horse again.

When we had a farm in Queensland, one of my daughters as a teenager had seven or eight horses at one stage. Horses were just beasts of burden to me, and I couldn't wait to get off a horse and get on a pushbike. It was ridiculous to ride a bike in those days when the country roads were unsealed, at best they were corrugated gravel roads.

I guess having it so tough, I really appreciate everything now. I can't throw things away. I'm a hoarder. I can still hear my mother's saying 'Waste not want not. Think of the poor people in China or India!' If there's a piece of fruit that's gone a bit ripe, I'll cut the ripe part off and eat the other part.

As for my wife, Jerri, when the children started to leave home she went to university. She got things she didn't have when she was young. She was 18 when we got married, and I was 22. She was a mother by 20 and I was a father at 24. The children just seemed to keep coming, which was the way it was in those days. I had four kids, and they all were girls.

Mr Lucky

I feel very privileged. What I do is so easy, because I've been doing it all my life. I think life is very unfair to a lot of people, I don't know why it's been so fair to me.

My theme is 'I can't get started'. It's a Bunny Berrigan trumpet solo from 1936, which I chose originally because it had a big fanfare, although I don't use it anymore. But the irony is the words 'I can't get started', when in fact 'I can't get stopped!' I've often thought my theme should have been 'Mr Lucky', but unfortunately Henry Mancini didn't write that until much later into my career, in about 1960!

I've been sacked a lot and I've had quite a few setbacks but I always come out on top. Mr Lucky.

I'm happy to have my family – I complain about them all the time, but they know I love them, and my grandchildren. We're booked to go to France for a month and all the family are coming over, including the family from England. I enjoy that. I'm a people person. I love people. I also have a lot of fun with the people at work and stir up people everywhere.

If you wanted to know what I'm proudest of, two things have been wonderful, more so than the Beatles tour. One was a friendship I had with Bill Cosby; it was great, before he was a mega star. He was only a super star then. When Bill's doing a show in America, if he knows there are people from Australia he'll go over and say, 'Are you from Sydney? Well, you say hello to my friend Bob Rogers!' That's nice. It's very hard to make contact with him today because he's so big. He's got this wall of managers, who won't let you near him.

The other thing I'm proud of was when I was in Hobart and I realised I had the facility to be a disc jockey. This is a very important part of the formulation of what I am – I started with nothing. For eight years I was nobody. I was exploited as people still are today, because I wanted to be in radio. I was doing afternoon Sundays, living in a converted garage in a guesthouse.

I subsequently got married at 22, and when I wanted Saturdays off because my wife was working – the station wouldn't give it to me. I had Tuesdays off. I used to do Saturday racing and Sunday afternoon, which were all spotted religious programs. There were spots in between the segments, and I said to the boss, 'Can I play special music?' He reluctantly agreed, and I went down to a rusty old freighter and saw the technician on board. He had a copy of a record, and I asked if I could have it. It was 'Riders in the Sky' by Vaughton Monroe.

You weren't supposed to take anything off the boat, but being Hobart it was always cold, and I had a jumper on. So I put the ten-inch shellac record under my jumper and played it on the radio. No one else had the song and suddenly I became well known as a disc jockey. I started to get sponsors and sold records for a record shop. I suddenly had about seven sponsors and the radio station still wouldn't give me any more money – £8.10 a week.

I have to keep reminding myself how old I am

I have to keep reminding myself how old I am, because I start talking about something and I can tell people haven't got the faintest idea what I'm talking about – because it goes back so far. I read a lovely quote:

'I'll never be an old man, to me old age is always 15 years older than I am.'

And that is true; I think we all come to terms with that.

There are a few other quotes, which I feel are so true.

'Whenever a man's friends begin to compliment him about looking young, he can be sure they think he's growing old.'

Then there is Samuel Johnson:

'There's a wicked inclination in most people, to suppose an old man decayed in his intellect. If a young, or middle-aged man leaving a company, does not remember where his hat is, it's nothing, but if the same inattention is discovered in a old man, people will shrug up their shoulders and say, His memory's going.'

Can Bob fix it? Yes, he can!

I'm a great mender of things. I'm not good, but I'm a great admirer of plumbers and people who can do things like that. All my daughters have what they call 'Bob jobs,' based on the old Scout thing. They'll ring up and say, 'I've got two Bob jobs for you,' so I go over and mend gates and put doors back on.

I like doing those physical things much more than sitting

at a computer. I'm not a good TV viewer because I grew up without watching television. I find it relaxing doing all those physical chores and would rather do something in the garden.

Hardware shops are part of my persona. I love hardware shops –

Bob the Builder! One of my daughters and her boyfriend extended my little shed out the back fulfiling the philosophy that every man needs a shed. I love my electric saw and all those other tools.

Obey your body

As you get older, you get to know your body and you obey your body. For instance, last Saturday night I had to do six hours straight because the new system has been giving us a lot of problems. Because I wake up at 5.30 or 6 and I didn't get home until almost 1 am the following day – Sunday, I was just totally exhausted. I turned down a dinner invitation and allowed myself time to recover and told them I wouldn't do it again next week.

You just obey your body.

I don't live in the past

I don't look very far ahead, but I don't live in the past.

I feel particularly sorry for those in my sort of business, that it is so much more difficult now – this terrible thing called economic rationalism which has come in everywhere; radio, TV, newspapers, banks. They just slash middle management, men of 50, and they all end up on the heap. I feel sorry for these people, a lot are now employed on contract, and they've got no sense of security. I just find it so tragic. I just think life batters some people around and they don't get the breaks.

It was easier in our day. It wasn't easy, but it was easier. There was a sense of security. If you lost one job, well you could see it coming and you could probably plan for another and to me security was the major influence in my life.

Education is terribly important

I see so many young men in their 30s who have no qualifications. They don't seem to have any idea of how they're going to provide for their children in the future. They have no qualifications and having kids is very expensive. I left school at 14, but you could afford to in my day. You had to work, to support the family. You paid board etc, just to help the family through. My wife and I were in our mid-30s before we ever went overseas – I was 39. I worry about their older years, and how they're going to take care of themselves financially.

I do think an education is terribly important. I know it's very tough, if you're young, with a girlfriend, working and doing a university course, but it's worth it for the long-term.

I'm just glad for every day

I don't want to attempt fate by suggesting how long I'm going to live for. I'm just glad for every day. I'd like to say that I greet every day with a positive attitude, but I don't, sometimes I'm cranky.

I think I got the attitude of being grateful from my mother. She was a good Christian woman. We were very proud of our mother. She was English. How she survived Donald, in Victoria on the edge of the Malley for 20 years, I shall never know. I hate the flatness and dryness of country towns; I even feel melancholy when I look at Afghanistan or Ethiopia, where there's all that dryness and no greenery. It was tough and Mum was the one who inspired us. When we walked off the farm, Mum was about 40 and went to work for the Brotherhood of St Lawrence and found her real metier. That was her life for the last ten years or so, and we are very proud of the fact that her ashes are buried in the crypt at St Peter's, the highest Anglican Church in Melbourne.

Is that all there is?

About 20 years ago, probably before I went into the rag

trade, I can remember thinking I was going to retire or something, I remember standing out the back and thinking, 'Is that all there is?" And I thought this is terrible, there's got to be something more to life. But I'm not looking for any magical answer. I'm totally unspiritual, totally unspiritual.

One of my daughters said to me, because she's looking for a spiritual answer to life, 'Dad, have you ever stopped to look into yourself?' and I said, 'No, darling, because there's nothing there!' And I seriously mean that. Jerri and I once went to Lhasa, capital of Tibet and I looked at these poor peasants, some of them with pads on their knees. They get down and they walk around on their knees, feeling this is how to get some salvation. It doesn't make sense.

Although I'm not particularly religious, I think I did point my finger at 'fate' or whatever you call God, as I see it. When I went in for cancer a lot of my listeners and some of my closest friends said prayers for me. I thought it was more the fickle finger of fate, because I had been cockily going on air saying I had never had a sickie in seven years; and God came down and said we'll show this fellow a trick or two!!

Energy is eternal delight
I feel I have a terrific attitude to life; I get a bit grumpy sometimes, but only when I take on too many things. I have to remind people that I do have a full time job. I get a lot of requests to do things and they're mostly for good causes. It can get a bit overwhelming and I really need a secretary to organise everything, but in the radio business you don't have a secretary unless you're an Alan Jones!

There is a good phrase, which I keep in the front of my appointment book. 'Energy is eternal delight.' That was something I didn't ever think of, until I was starting to get older.

I also like this wonderful quote:

'A man isn't old until regrets take the place of dreams.' I think that's wonderful. And I quote this to my daughters; 'The mind is its own place, and in itself can make a heaven of hell, or a hell of heaven.' That's attitude.

Chapter 12

Karl Stockhausen

Gunther Karl Stockhausen was born in Hamburg in 1930, and in 1955 decided to emigrate to Australia to gain overseas experience. He found work as a vineyard hand at Lindemans' vineyard in Pokolbin NSW and helped occasionally with office duties. He then transferred to Lindemans' head office in Sydney where he again performed clerical and accounting duties. During this time he assisted or relieved the manager at the Ben Ean winery in the Hunter Valley and gained further experience in winemaking and vintage operations. In 1959, Lindemans appointed Karl as Manager/Winemaker at their Ben Ean winery. He married Peggy at that time, and in 1961 their daughter Toni was born. Peggy died in 1978, and at the end of 1979 Karl was appointed manager of Leo Buring's Chateau Leonay in the Barossa Valley. Karl then went on to work in Lindemans head office Sydney as Brand Manager, Fine Wines Manager and PR Manager. In 1990, after 35 years with Lindemans, he was made redundant and Karl has since worked as consultant to a number of vineyards, particularly with Briar Ridge Vineyard.

Karl is very respected in the wine industry. He is well known as a wine judge at both the Hunter Valley and the Mudgee Wine Shows. Since 1996 he has been chairman of the tasting panel of the Australia Wine Selectors and he is a foundation member of the Australian Society of Wine Education.

Today at 75 Karl still consults to vineyards, conducts seminars, is actively involved with judging and tasting panels, goes skiing (which he didn't learn until age 59), helps his partner Julie with her café, drives the fire truck, and fights the fierce Australian bushfires.

I can't stay in bed too long, got to be up and at it. Most days I'll be up by 7 am, have a cup of tea, make some breakfast, only very light, generally only a bit of fruit and yoghurt maybe.

After my partner Julie leaves for work, I start washing the tea towels for the café, then I do whatever has to be done – water the veggie garden, run into town, do some banking, do the mail, and Monday and Tuesday do Julie's books for the week before and enter it in the PC. Maybe do some ordering for the café and the wages.

I'll have a bit of lunch, do the shopping for the next week, take that down to the café, and there's not much left of the day. If the weather permits I'll come home and do some work outside, work in the garden or whatever. About one day a week I also work as Chairman of the tasting panel with the Australian Wine Selectors in Newcastle. I get up early and head off to Newcastle and do tastings and discussion all day.

Other days I'm still working consulting with other wineries. Particularly with Briar Ridge, Wandin Valley, Allendale and some others. That takes another day or so a week. I give them advice, have a look at the vines and tell them when to get them in, etc.

I don't have morning or afternoon tea, lunch generally for me is rye bread sandwiches with a bit of cheese, salami, or whatever is there, and a glass of milk. Years ago when you couldn't buy rye bread I used to bake my own.

I don't go out of my way to have something because it's good for you. I never have, but at the same time, I like fruit. I don't have sugar. Whenever someone comes and wants a cup of tea or coffee, I have to start looking for some sugar. I just don't want it. Every now and then I want something sweet and if you gave me a nice box of chocolates, I can eat the whole lot in one go. No problem. But I don't buy cakes or sweets, I don't even think about buying them.

For dinner we have a lot of variation. I don't eat as much meat as I used to, but I do like my little bit of lamb or cutlets, chicken, and every now and then a bit of beef. I like fish and eat it one or two times a week. Everything is generally grilled, and we do a lot on the barbeque. In winter I might cook stews, meats, with herbs, like Osso bucco. I've got to have my greens and I eat a lot of salads.

Occasionally we might have a spaghetti dish with a cream sauce. Generally I don't eat chips, but if Julie comes home and we want a drink before dinner, we might have some chips or a few nuts. Nuts more likely than chips, but it's not a daily routine. You go out for lunch or dinner and you see all these people having a bowl of deep-fried chips, even before they have dinner. If we go to have a cheap meal at the club or somewhere, virtually all my chips go back. I'll eat the fish and have a couple of chips and all the rest go back. It's not that I don't eat any fat, I just don't want it. I don't have fast food, hamburgers etc and only occasionally pizza, preferably home made.

Wine is good for you
Rarely I have desserts, but I always have wine, plenty of red, whatever fits in, maybe even a glass of bubbly. I've been regularly drinking wine virtually all my life.

In my childhood we had Sunday dinner, which was invariably some fatty greasy pork, which I as a child hated. But you had to eat it, 'Its good for you!' I can still remember the days where you weren't allowed to cut off the fat, and it would almost make me vomit. Nevertheless we still had our bits of fruit, banana, etc. We didn't eat white bread, we always had rye bread or at least bread that was multi-grain, and a banana sandwich was always my favourite.

We had some very lean years during the war, went quite hungry and ate whatever came along, which wasn't much. After that, when I was working I'd eat in the canteen. It was customary to have your main hot dinner at mid-day and at night you just had a bit of bread with sausage or cheese. My diet growing up was richer, with much more fat, and sauces. Now I eat plenty of salads, with herbs, tomatoes, beans, potatoes and carrots from the garden.

I don't do really any exercise for the sake of exercise
I don't do really any exercise for the sake of exercise, but I do a lot of physical work around the property. Even when I built my house, I helped the builders and virtually did all of the painting outside. I keep working, and there's always physical work to do. I think I'm a bit of a handyman – I like to fix things. I like working with wood and built an entertainment unit for my stereo.

The volunteer fire brigade has kept me fit, especially of recent years. No sooner have my overalls dried than somebody rings up and says we need a crew. And we go out again. It's terrible; sometimes it goes on for weeks. You're not allowed to go out without training and I've got a licence to drive the fire truck. You need to know what hose to use, how to handle it, use an axe, use a rake and a hoe, and know how to operate the radio.

The challenge with the fire brigade is that I might be doing something when the phone rings and someone asks you get out to the truck. You drop everything, get into your overalls and take off. And you never know when you're coming back. Apart from bush fires we also get called for other things, like one day a fellow's car burst into flames on the side of the road.

How old would you be if you didn't know how old you are?
People say I don't look my age. I don't, but I don't feel like a 20 year-old either, nor do I want to. It wasn't all that happy a time for me. Invariably I meet a man, respectful because he's my senior, and then I find out I'm ten years older than he is! When I met Julie, (she's 26 years younger than me) I thought she was closer to my age. Her mother said sometime fairly early in the piece, 'How do you feel with a young girl like that?' I hadn't really thought about it.

I've never really thought about age. My daughter gave me a

magnet for the fridge for my birthday – 'How old would you be if you didn't know how old you are?' When you're 15 you think 20 is pretty old, and when you're 25 you think, my God, he's 50 already. And then when you get near 50 you think 60's not that old!

I play golf sometimes, but there's not much exercise in it. I used to play squash, but all the guys I used to play with have all fallen by the wayside. I do what I like to do. I go skiing and travelling, hopefully at least once a year. The last few years we've been down in Thredbo doing wine dinners and wine classes and it always left the morning to go skiing and that was great. I was around 59 when I first started skiing. I noticed a sign and it said after 65 you can ski for nothing. I thought, 'I'm looking forward to that.' Now I get the lift tickets for a very reduced price. They think you're too old to ski!

If you drink as much wine as I do, you won't have any problems!

I've had a bad back for a long time, but it's not handicapping me in any way. I haven't had any other problems at all. If you drink as much wine as I do, you won't have any problems!

I expect to live as least as long as my mother, she died at 79 – actually I think I might outlast her. I know I will die one day and I just hope that it happens suddenly, bang I'm gone. I hate the thought of lingering on with something like my wife did. She kept on very optimistic and positive, but she was suffering with cancer for something like ten years and it just dragged on and on, with different treatments and operations.

I don't take any medications; I'm always amazed when I see people with five pills before they have breakfast!

Stress, what's that?
I might have been stressed at some time, but now I'm pretty relaxed with everything. The only stress that I can really think of was financial, early in my working life. When I arrived in Australia I had £5 in my pocket. When I worked as the

winery manager here in the Hunter Valley, I had a wife and a daughter and the money was sufficient, but that was all. It would just keep us going, there wasn't really anything to be saved. In the beginning it was from hand to mouth, there was never anything left over. As things got better we bought a house, and from then on things relaxed a bit more.

Now I am relaxed all the time. I had a girlfriend in Adelaide once who was a yoga teacher, so I got a bit of meditation from her. I don't consciously sit down and meditate, but often I just lie on the floor, no longer than ten minutes, not a sleep, but just totally relaxed – then I'm off back to work. I find that refreshing. They say Napoleon did the same thing, but Bonaparte used to sit in the middle of the battle and fall asleep on his horse! I also find it relaxing to just sit on the mower, cut some grass, or do some ironing. These things are so monotonous you have to relax.

I don't think about ageing

It doesn't occur to me. There are some restrictions. I can't see as well as I used to, so I wear glasses. I don't worry about it. That's fine. It makes me see better and I can actually read. Good.

When the time comes, as I sometimes have trouble hearing when there's a lot of background noise, I will have no hesitation in wearing a hearing aid. That, too, is fine. On the other hand, I wouldn't think of cosmetic surgery or facelifts, I'd rather have a few wrinkles than look like some of these people who look like they're wearing masks.

No Regrets

With hindsight, you probably think there are all sorts of things you should have done. At the time I did what looked appropriate and right, I don't regret anything and I don't think I would do anything different. The saying 'If I had known then what I know now I would have...' just doesn't work.

Your Health is the Most Important Thing

Health is the most important thing, I like to stay healthy, hate it when I've got a cold. I've never really been sick apart from the normal colds. Occasionally I'll wake up in the morning and feel lousy, so then I hibernate or just do nothing all day. Flop on the floor, wake up, have a glass of water and the next day I'm fine.

If I feel I'm getting a sore throat or something I take a bit of ascorbic acid (vitamin C) dissolved in water, I'll take it throughout the day. Sometimes I don't catch it early enough but usually I keep doing it, and two days later there is no sign of a cold. It's gone.

Drink wine, but don't smoke!

I have found that you cannot give advice to younger people. They have to do something and make their own mistakes, and only then will they learn. If there is any recommendation I would give people, apart from drinking wine, it would be don't smoke. I used to smoke very heavily, my wife smoked and my mother-in-law who was living with us.

I started when I was about 18. My father was a very heavy smoker and as a young fellow I smoked a cigarette a day. I went on holiday with my friend and we gave up smoking while we were away. I got home and proudly told my father. He said, 'That's good,' and offered me a cigarette! I started again and from that moment on, it slowly got worse. When I got to Australia I was smoking a packet a day. Eventually it got to the point 30 years ago, where if I wanted to make a phone call, I'd first have a cigarette. If the phone rang I'd light another cigarette. Over a pack a day. It was ridiculous, and all the money I was wasting! It's not good for you anyway, so why do it?

It wasn't easy. My experience was that you get a craving every now and again, and shortly after you give smoking away, that is fairly frequent. None of the cravings last, they are very short and all you have to do is say, 'I'm not.' Then its fine and it comes again. The longer the time goes on the longer the spells of good in between. I would say to myself, 'No I won't, 12 months time maybe, but not now.' While I was giving up I did have one funny experience. I woke up one morning and I was very annoyed with myself because I had had a cigarette the night before, but I had only dreamt that I had smoked a cigarette! It took about 12 months before I could say that I wasn't thinking about it any more.

I've never taken any other drugs. Once in Germany where there were opium dens, a close friend said, 'What do you think? I would really like to try it, just to see.' I said, 'I'm not, I'm scared. From what I read and what I know, I feel I don't want to try and I don't want to see what its like.' He said, 'Mate – you're strong enough to try it and then say forget it.' But I didn't want to do that.

I learnt how to use a computer at about 62
To keep mentally alert, I read the paper and I play with the computer and that's quite challenging. I'd like to do a computer course. Every now and then I have a go and want to learn French. After several weeks of trying, I give that away until the next time.

I speak German, but I don't use it at all. If I have to speak to some German visitors I'm suddenly confronted with trying to find the right terms because they didn't exist when I left Germany – for example, television.

I have no particular spiritual views on life. Theoretically I'm still a Lutheran. I wouldn't call myself an atheist, but I don't believe there is anything there. People like to believe, to hang onto something. Good on them. If all the evils, all the nasties that are happening are approved by whoever is up there, well, he ought to be shot!

My philosophy is whatever you do, do it in moderation except wine!

In the next 20 years I want to keep doing much the same. I just sort of carry on and carry on. I want to keep moving and doing. One thing I don't want to do

is sit around and do nothing. As long as people want me for consulting I'll be there. I never think about age. I just keep at it, keep doing the things I love to do. I've never held back.

Chapter 13

Bryce Courtenay

Bryce Courtenay is the best-selling author of books like 'The Power of One', 'April Fools Day', 'A Recipe for Dreaming', The Family Frying Pan', 'Smokey Joe's Café', and 'The Potato Factory.' He is one of Australia's leading authors, and an international star. His books are made into films and he has sold more than four million books in Australia alone. His first novel, 'The Power of One', has been translated into 11 languages, and has now sold over two million copies. The movie of the book has been an international success.

Bryce was born illegitimately in 1933 in South Africa and spent his early childhood years in a small town deep in the heart of the Lebombo Mountains. He grew up among farm folk and the African people. At the age of five he was sent to an orphanage.

He came to Australia in 1958, a year later began his advertising career with McCann Erickson, and became Australia's youngest creative director at the age of 31. After ten years he joined J. Walter Thompson as its creative director where he remained for a further five years before leaving to start his own agency which he sold to the international BBDO Group. In 1987 Bryce joined George Patterson advertising as a creative director. He retired at the end of 1993 to write full-time.

Bryce was invited by the Chinese Government to give the first series of lectures on the subject of advertising and free enterprise. Bryce has lectured on the power of the individual to achieve any end purpose in UK, USA, NZ, South Africa, and Canada, and is regarded as one of the top five speakers in Australia.

He has won most of the local and international advertising awards and in addition won a gold medal for the best documentary at the 1984 New York Film Festival. In 1995 Bryce was awarded the Order of Australia.

In addition 'Mr Energy' is a keen fitness enthusiast, having run 39 marathons and 10 ultra marathons. Now Bryce is easing up, sleeping up to five hours night, and only running half marathons, a mere 21 kilometres!!!

What I do each day depends very much on what is happening during the day. If it's a writing day it's quite different to the other days. A writing day begins very early. It generally begins between 4.30 and 4.45am. I get up and do an hour and a half exercise. I used to only do an hour's running, but now that I walk more than I run, I do half an hour's running and an hour's walking. That seems to be about the equivalent of running hard for an hour, but having had an arthroscopy recently; I've taken to walking. Hopefully I'll get back to do more running.

Then it's breakfast by 6 or 6.30 and I'll sit down and work for 12 hours straight. I don't get up, nothing. I don't even have lunch. I have a large bottle of water next to the computer and about every hour, if I can remember, I stretch. There are days when I sit down at say 6.30, and think it's time to stretch and I look and it's three o'clock in the afternoon! I haven't actually spoken to anybody or done anything, just kept writing right through. I stop at six o'clock always, when my alarm goes off. It doesn't matter where I am, even mid-sentence, I'll stop.

Hopefully by then I will have written 8,000 -10,000 words and I'll probably see my partner for the first time that day. I have a study upstairs, and she may have yelled to me goodbye, or I may have heard the car go out as she goes out, but that's it. So after six I sit down, have a glass of wine and we'll talk a bit and catch up with the day. We have dinner about seven and then the evening is free to do whatever we want to do. When we lived in Sydney we'd go to a concert or the theatre. We have a fairly active night social life because when you work those kinds of hours, you need to have some sort of relief that takes you right away from it. I spend a great deal of time on my own, obviously.

When I'm not writing, well, that's an entirely different business. I get up about half-past six, which is sheer luxury, and I do the same exercise again. Occasionally I take a day's rest, like on a Sunday. I will sleep in and maybe not do a full hour and a half's hard exercise.

A non-writing day is a very ordinary day, we go to concerts, we go to theatre, we go the movies, and I go and teach in America for two weeks of the year, which is fun. And we go on at least a three-week holiday, somewhere exotic like the Silk Road in Pakistan, Antarctic, Africa, Patagonia, the Himalayas or somewhere like that. This year we're probably going to Alaska, and South America after that. It generally involves for me, rather than my partner, a pack. I like to have a week of where I'll actually sleep in the open or in a tent.

Breakfast is generally two pieces of toast and a cup of coffee. I haven't had butter now, for probably five years, but I'll probably put a bit of Philadelphia cream on my toast with a bit of vegemite. As a special treat, on the weekends I have bacon and eggs.

Lunch when I'm writing is probably nothing. When I'm not writing at most it would be fruit or a salad. Dinner is a salad with fish or steak and sometimes potatoes. We have fish at least three times a week. I have a partner who is very health conscious and she watches me like a hawk.

Ideally I should be ten and a half stone, about 71 kg. I have great difficulty keeping it around there. It generally creeps up to about 75kg when I'm writing. It's just sitting for those long hours, even though you've done an hour and a half exercise every day. It's a sedentary sort of existence and it's very hard.

According to my partner, I eat a big meal at night, but I don't think I do. She keeps the size down. For instance, the steak is the size of a pack of cards as she calls it. I never have desserts. I don't have a sweet tooth so it's not a problem for me, but I might have fruit. I eat a lot of fruit and a lot of vegies. Everything is grilled, nothing is pan-fried. But those are just fundamentals, I've been doing that for 25 years. Two glasses of wine a night would be max for me except if I'm going to a party or something like that. It's always white wine because the red affects my sinuses.

Every day I take two fish capsules, Glucosamine for my joints and in the winter Echinacea.

I very seldom have a beer or any spirits. I don't drink enough water, probably four or five glasses a day. Nothing like enough. Coffee three a day, or two coffees and a cup of tea. I have to have a coffee first thing in the morning after a run. When we lived in Sydney, because my routine was so regular, at 6.30am the coffee shop would have it all packed up and waiting!

Upper body strength is critical, as you're getting older

We usually go to the gym three times a week, both of us, and this is very important for older people. It's more important almost than the aerobic exercise, not that anything is more important than the aerobic exercise. Most old people say, 'Yeah I walk,' but they forget about the upper body and upper body strength is critical, as you're getting older. It's what keeps your frame up, it stops the hunch you see, it improves the way you walk, everything. I do weights three times a week, I'm not trying to prove anything and just use good steady weights on a program. That has helped me. I cannot tell you how important it is, especially for somebody like me who's had a spinal fusion. It's sensational; if you're going to be older and you don't do upper body strength, you can be fit but you can still be in a lot of pain. You can even do exercises in your own bedroom if you want.

A gym's a good idea because it's a social exercise – you go out, you're forced to do things, You have a routine, the machines are there for you to use. You can't make any excuses. It has a sense of occasion. From my observation, one of the things that concerns me about older people, is they lose their sense of occasions. They settle down into a routine that's easy and that accommodates whatever aches and pains they've got. And they don't create for themselves what I call the 'daily surprises'. Something that you actually look forward to doing. That is nevertheless routine, but gets you out of the house. It makes you do something which is good for you, intellectually and from a health point of view. Very often the two are very closely attached. Intellectual health and physically health are very closely aligned. The one works very well with the other. You can be terribly healthy, but with nothing going on in your head, you can be very unwell.

I will live until I die
I don't really think about ageing too much, most people I'm sure say the same thing, but I genuinely don't. I was born in Africa and the concept of mortality is something I've known since a very small child. It's been something that I've accepted as a daily occurrence in my environment. I know that inevitably my death will come. I have one single premise that I make and that is, I will live until I die and when that is, is unimportant. I don't wake up and think, 'Oh my God I'm getting old, it's hurting', because you do wake up with pains you didn't have the night before, but that's life. I think you learn to live with that. You learn to live with the fact that you are getting older.
I actually have quite enjoyed the process of getting older because you have fewer hassles in your head. I think you are a little wiser and you've wised up to the fact that quarrelling about silly things is stupid. There's lot of things that come with age, with maturity any way. I think maturity is probably a better word than age, because age is a state of being whereas maturity is a state of having arrived. And that becomes a very important idea. You're mature enough to handle decisions, situations, that 10 or 15 or 20 years ago would have hassled you enormously or created enormous crisis.

Ageing is the word 'age' and ageing is viewed largely as crisis. In other words, if we are worried about something we age far more quickly and incrementally than we would do if we're not worried about something. If we're neurotic we age more quickly than if we are phlegmatic, and in effect the whole concept of maturity is a concept of intelligent ageing. It's a way of foreclosing on the stupid things, the silly things and the daily quarrels. The you said, I said, nonsense that goes on between most couples.

It's coming to terms with the fact that you can't have sex every day, but you can certainly have it twice a week. That's an important concept. Lots of men walk around and they become impotent just worrying about the fact that they're not the rams that they used to be. There's a lovely old saying about menopause in men. When I do a talk I say, 'Don't wait to do the things that you're going to do in life, when menopause comes...' You always get that grin, because men think it's something that happens to women. I say, 'Why do you think it's called menopause, not called women-o-pause? You can always tell when a male has hit menopause because he can't see his willy and the busiest part of his body is his elbow!' That gets a bit of a chuckle.

One day I was doing a conference for the Wound Carers. (I am a patron of the Wound Carers Association of Australia) I only take patronages of things that nobody else would dream of doing because wound carers are about bed sores and suchlike. I did this little menopause thing and got the usual bit of a titter. Afterwards a doctor came up to me and said, 'Oh you've got it all wrong,' and I thought, 'Oh God, here we go. I'm going to get a lecture on male menopause!' 'It's only a joke' I said to him. He said, 'No, no, you've got it all wrong. Male menopause is the three nevers. Never pass a urinal. Never waste an erection. Never trust a fart!'

Now I've reached those three stages. It's a lovely piece of understanding of life. Your bladder doesn't work as well as it ought to. It's a lovely surprise when you've got an erection, and you've got to watch yourself in the other department.

Always do just a little more than you think you can do.
I'm probably going to live three days over 95, because I've always had a credo in my life. If you're going to run a race where everyone else is in it, say it's a marathon. When you hit the winning post, run another 150 yards just to prove to yourself that you can. Always do just a little more than you think you can do. I know I can make 95, so I'll do three more days.

It's difficult for an author to have goals in the sense of most people, because each time you write something, it is a brand new work of creation. It's beginning out of nothing. You carve something out of nothing and in the end you have created a small universe of your own. That's what an author or an artist does, unlike a singer who will lose her voice. My written voice is likely to stay with me for a long, long time. Your goal is to write as intelligently and as well as you've done in the past 14 or so novels you've written. I think I've probably got 27 in my head – another 13. That brings me up to the age of 83, but I'll probably slow down a little bit because you do. Maybe that will take me right up to age 90!

I am in the process right now of building the garden I've always wanted. You think a garden isn't going to take you that long, well mine is. Mine's going to take me probably ten years to build. It's about two and a half acres. It involves seven ponds and thousands of plants. That's going to take years to mature. I'm doing it myself, that's why it's going to take so long. I don't want somebody coming along, and there's an instant garden, apart from the bulldozers which are going to shape the land. Yes, I'm going to do it all myself. That means I'm going to make the walls, do the stonework and lay the paths. It's going to take a long time, but it is a labour of love. You have created again, something brand new.

In the Zulu language there are the three ages of man and they go like this. A man is complete when he has planted a tree, had a son, (in Zulu culture, daughters don't count), and created a story to sit in with the stories of the tribe. If you translate that literally, it's to have a garden, to have a son, (I had three) and to write a book. I've done that cycle, but the garden is the last one I want to do. I know exactly what it will look like. It will be incredibly beautiful and restful. People can come and sit there, read and love it. Hopefully when I die it will be left to writers and artists, people who need a rest.

Old age is when you stop to learn

My goals haven't really changed in essence. I don't think there is a time in your life where you give up doing what you do, particularly if you're somebody like me who's a creative person. You can't turn that tap off. It doesn't turn off. You don't say, 'Now I'm going to stop being creative, stop dreaming, stop thinking'. You can't do that and yet I watch people doing it. They actually turn off the tap saying, 'Too old to do that now', and the tap gets turned off and turned off until it's a trickle, then the odd drop and then finally one day, the tap stops dripping entirely and they die.

I think old age is when you stop to learn. When you can no longer absorb something which is fresh and new, that will allow you to change your perspective or your mind. That can happen quite early in life. I know a teenager of 19 who's closed down completely and she's an old woman already. 70 isn't very old. I've got another 25 years to go. I don't think of 70 as being an age at all. It has no significance.

Middle age is where you reach a level of maturity

Middle age is that point where you start to mature, where your judgement arrives. It doesn't have a definition. It's not fixed at 50 or anything like that. It says my judgement now is such that I cannot only appreciate something, but I understand why I appreciate it. There are the jumble years where you listen to music that doesn't really have to make a lot of sense, it's just noise. Where you read books, which don't have to make sense, where you look at movies that don't have to make a lot of sense. Slowly you separate those strands and you build for yourself a kind of intellectual citadel, where you know what things touch you and are meaningful to you, and why they are meaningful to you. When that comes, that's the first mark of maturity. It doesn't mean you have superior tastes to anybody else. It just means that you are comfortable with the reasons why you do things. You don't just do them automatically; you're not forced by society to do them. You know when to object to something that is politically wrong, even if it's against what the majority thinks. That's all maturity.

It's understanding, 'What do I really think about this?' Not, 'That's OK,' or 'That's not OK'. But 'Why, why do I think it's not OK?' to be able to work that out in your head. Here are my reasons, now debate me. Give me yours and I'll give you mine. If you can convince me, I'll be only too happy to change. But I know why I don't want that to happen. Knowing the why is the hardest part of everything. That's maturity and that is middle age.

Somebody has to do it, it might as well be you

Teenagers are confused, scared, worried about life, quite apart from the fact that they may act irrationally or irresponsibly. Those fears are latent and they really do worry about how they're going to compete. How they're going to get involved with society.

I had a very difficult life in the beginning. I spent some time in an orphanage and I was born illegitimately. Things didn't come all that easily to me, we were very poor, but I had a grandfather who had a rose garden and he was passionate about roses. As a small kid about seven or eight I used to have to dig holes for these roses, because we were much too poor to have an African gardener. It was very hard work up in the mountains. It can be anything up to 150° F or 45°C, hard work digging there as a small kid. I'd be pruning the roses and my grandfather would stop and light his pipe.

He'd say, 'Well then lad, what are we going to do when we grow up?' Being just a little kid, it was during the war and I wanted to be a spitfire pilot. I'd read Biggles books etc and I said, 'I'm going to kill Germans.' He'd go puff, puff, puff, on his pipe and say, 'Well then lad, somebody has to do it, it might as well be you.'

A simple little phrase, but it occurred to me, even at the age of seven, where I had no chance, I was sent back into an orphanage, which was closer to a reform school than an orphanage really. I was going nowhere, there was nothing that meant I wasn't going to be digging ditches all my life, except for this little credo 'Somebody has to do everything, it might as well be you!'

At 11 I won a scholarship out of 3,000 kids who applied. This kid without a pair of shoes, in an orphanage, won it. Suddenly I was capitulated into a school for millionaires, the poshest private school in southern Africa. All my life whenever something seemed more difficult or bigger than I could handle, this phrase would come back to me and it'd say, 'Somebody has to do it. It might as well be you.' It's a simple little idea but it's an idea that has ultimate meaning, when you think about it. Every generation has to fill every slot there is in society. It becomes a question of your choosing which of those slots you want to fill. The only limitations really are yourself.

The journey is a splendid idea, the destination is just another place to be.

If you just say to yourself, 'It might as well be me.' That always suggests, that's where you want to go. You may say the difficulties are much too hard, I might never get there. But the moment you say, 'It might as well be me,' you've actually committed yourself to something you really would like to do. Once that happens you can do it. I believe that you actually can do anything you set your mind to doing. The costs maybe more than you're prepared to pay. That's up to you, but it can actually be achieved. People who spend all their time motivating other people always fill the first part of the sentence. 'You can do anything you want to do,' but not the second part. The second part is: 'If you're prepared to pay the price, the cost.' The cost's always there. Yes, it's true but it has a price. Once you say, 'It might as well be me', you take on the price not the target. Then you have to start sorting out what the price is going to be to get there. I talk to a lot of teenagers and I talk to them in those terms. Rather than, 'You're the best, you can do this, you're amazing, you're a generation that has everything.' It doesn't help a kid at all. But to say, 'Yeah, it's a hard grind, but the learning part is the nicer part. The getting there is far nicer than having gotten there.' The journey is a splendid idea; the destination is just another place to be.

Your body is going to have to last you probably 90 years, so look after it.

Your body is going to have to last you probably 90 years, so don't be silly and do things to it that are going to curtail that. Your best years are from 50 on, even that might seem amazing to a lot of people younger. Look after your body. Don't be stupid, don't become a fanatic. There's an old Victorian adage and it goes like this: Moderation in all things, even in moderation.

When you get to your 40s, and I hate these demarcations, the advice has to be specified by gender. If female, you are facing the first real crisis in your life, which is that your children are now getting towards independence so that your natural function of motherhood is beginning to close down. You now have to look at yourself as an entirely different human being. You're no longer going to be the mother that had total preoccupation with her children and their up-bringing. Although they're going to worry you for the rest of your life, and they're going to be a pain forever, for you, yourself, a metamorphosis is about to take place.

As a generalisation, you'll find that motherhood has created a whole period of bad habits and one of them is to put yourself last. You eat the scraps and you put on weight and you smoke possibly, maybe you're a bit neurotic and you've got a short temper with the kids. These are the downsides, the upsides are that you've learnt to be wise with your children. You've guided them through, but always you'll find you've placed yourself in a negative position for all those years.

It is time for a major overhaul when you hit mid-40s, and that is to look at yourself and say, 'This is a new human being, that has to learn a whole new set of habits and one of them is to put herself first.' Because if you don't, the old habits will continue and as your children get older they will still depend on you. They will have expectations of you that are unfair, that will deny you the life you're entitled to have. Very much fitness comes into it, very much a career comes into it, or at least a very involved hobby, charity or whatever, depending on what your circumstances are. Some involvement that takes you out of the house. That gets you into a life, a circle and an environment. That is hugely important. I love to see some of them going back to uni for instance, or going to uni for the first time. That's the kind of metamorphosis that I'm talking about. Now it's my turn and it's a nice 'my turn', because you've now got a bit of maturity. You may still be preoccupied with your looks, but you're not competing with 21 year olds any more. You're happy that you have another 40 years at least, ahead of you.

You've only reached at the very least the middle of your life and yet you've achieved all of those things expected of a female gender, you've created a new generation. But now you're free. That freedom is a very precious idea and not to use it, is a kind of crime against yourself. It is a shame when people don't use that time.

In his 40s there is a question of fitness; a man's got to start thinking about his diet, he's got to start trimming down
The male at 40 has just about grown up. I believe he should start seriously taking over the parental role. Now he's got teenage kids or late teens and they need some very real

guidance. It is here that the father plays a far more significant part than he may have played in the first 10 or 15 years of the child's life. Now he should play the dominant role. It's not a long role to play – five or six years maybe, but a very important one for him to play in the life of his children, male and female. To see his kids through those tender teenage years, late teenage years, early 20s, the confusion time.

He is now, in a strange sense, better equipped to advise his children than the mother. He's been out in the world; he hasn't had the responsibilities of the day-to-day bringing up of his kids. I'm talking about a fairly traditional family here. You still get working mothers, but again, a working mother is still doing twice the work of a working father. He's still allowed to go out there while she's housebound, even if she's working.

Again there is a question of fitness, because by 40 he's given up regular sport, if he's stupid. He's put on weight; he's drinking too much beer. We're averaging these things. It's all generalisation. He's got to start thinking about his diet, he's got to start trimming down. He's got to start to think about competing with his kids to stay with them, because that's his job, and getting himself a life.

His career should be at a stage where he knows where he's going and where he can plot it reasonably well. If he's not happy 40 is the time for a male to change his career, not 50. He's still young enough to change the career; he's still young enough to learn. He's still young enough to be accepted in the work environment. And he's still young enough to get some traction; so that his superannuation is going to be intact by the time he hits 60.

We think life is about having things, where in fact life is about doing things

Stress, trying to think if I get it? I don't stress very easily. I've had too tough a life to stress easily. One of the joys of having had my kind of background is that you've been everywhere and you know what the consequences are of starting at the bottom and then getting kicked, picking yourself up and dusting yourself off. It's pretty hard to stress somebody like that.

We are always stressed about all the wrong things – we get stressed about the future, we get stressed about what will happen to us, we get stressed about superannuation and we get stressed about relationships. I tend not to join in fights if I can help it. Most problems with relationships is that each wants to own a part of something, within the family environment. I want to own this aspect of our life, and you own that aspect, and there are clashes.

I went through stress before it was known as stress, you just thought; well that's what life is all about. Life is tough. It is tough and anyone who thinks it isn't tough is silly. We have come to expect things to be easy, but they're not. They're never going to be easy. We always thought that once we had lots of money, or the rent was paid, or the mortgage was in control, or a dozen other things were taken care of, we wouldn't have stress. We have stress because we think that life is about having things, where in fact life is about doing things. People get enormously stressed about having things and it has nothing to do with life. If they got stressed with doing things, they would be far less stressed, because you'd say we going to do this and we're going to do that. You can plan and you can enjoy it. But we're going to have this; we're going to have that! Somebody gets it before you and you're stressed because you're competitive. That's nonsense.

To be helpful to yourself is to be physically fit and intellectually fit
Relationships are the most important. Always, people are more important than anything else you can do, and your mind. I would take my life if I lost my intellect. If I lost my capacity to think straight I would immediately take my life. I think the concept of dementia or Alzheimer's would be just too horrible to contemplate, because then I don't want to exist.

I have one weakness, in that I never want to be a burden on anybody. Some people say, 'Relax, let me do it for you.' I'm just one of those people who doesn't want to be any kind of a burden. I came into this world alone and it's been that way pretty well until I found a gorgeous partner. The idea of being helpless is too appalling for words, but then again it's a preoccupation, which most people reaching 70 and over seem to have. I don't want to be helpless. You have to be helpful to yourself, in order not to be helpless.

To be helpful is to be physically fit and intellectually fit. Intellectual health is enormously important. The two things are synergistic. They can't be separated. You can't be a mental slob and fit. It just doesn't work. You remain interested. One of the best ways to remain interested is so simple, read the newspaper every day and read it properly. Get angry, read the letters column. Find out about what other people are thinking. Read books, books keep you hugely intellectually fit. It doesn't matter what kind of books they are, novels, biographies, how to's, whatever, but read. Reading is an active participation. Your mind is actively reading, whereas television is passive, nothing is happening, or adding to your intellectual health. It's not making you think. Learning to listen is also a very important idea.

What's important is to know all the functions that will serve you intelligently

I'm not worried about keeping up to date with technology. I bought probably the first home computer out. It was roughly the size of a dining table and cost me $12,000! So I've been using computers for about 20 years. I can send emails and do the web. I can write a book on a computer, but that's the limit. I can run the tape, the video and the DVD, but I don't want to know any more than that. I don't have any desire to do anything else with that piece of technology. I think what's important is to know all the functions that will serve you intelligently, rather than those you don't have to have. Like a phone that can tap messages out, take photos.

That's kids' stuff, the kids love it and it's terrific.
Every now and then the computer goes bung and I pick up the phone and call somebody, I don't sit there for four hours working it out. Somebody comes in and five minutes later it's working. I don't feel I'm an idiot because I called him in. I haven't got time for that. My life is too busy doing other things.

I don't think of relaxation as a reward for having done something else

Nobody's relaxed all the time, unless you're a sponge, but I think I'm not het up a lot. I get annoyed about injustice; I get annoyed about greed; I get annoyed about racism. I'm likely to be the guy, who if somebody is calling somebody a f... Nigger, will go up to him, even if he's 7ft tall, and get smashed in the mouth for telling him off. I've done that before and been hit. Unfairness, racism, greed, cruelty to women, all those things get me hugely upset.

I am 'unwound' most of the time. I don't think of relaxation as a reward for having done something else. It's difficult, I'm a writer; my life is inside my head. My universe is in there. When I stop writing after those twelve-hour days that's relaxation time. I shut the door to my writing family, those characters in my book, have a shower and sit down. That's relax time and I'm back into what I call the first world.

I did meditate for years. I can now do it so automatically and often do when I'm writing. I can do four hours writing without hearing a phone or a noise because I get so deeply down. It's what used to be known as 'down to a level'. You get down to a level where nothing occurs except your thought process and I can do that almost instantly. But it took ten years to do that. I used to meditate for 40 minutes a day every day, but I don't any more, it just isn't necessary.

I sorted everything out in those three months

I was born with an arrhythmia, but I've run 39 marathons and about ten ultras. I have my heart checked every year, the arrhythmia's still there but it hasn't progressed. The answer is I don't run a marathon at 70; it's just not intelligent. I run half a marathon. The last one was the Sydney Half Marathon about a year ago.

I broke my back as a kid and nobody told me. I suffered hugely from backache, but again there was nobody to moan at, so you can't moan. I just accepted that as part of what happened. Sometimes I'd be in a meeting and it would just hit me and they'd cart me off in an ambulance. Then they discovered that I had five vertebrae which had worn out.

Today it's a fairly normal process to do a spinal fusion with a laser beam, but then I was in a plaster cast from my neck to my knees for three months. It wasn't a lot of fun but it was good time to sort myself out at the critical age of 50. I went in, I smoked 100 cigarettes a day, and I was a heavy drinker. When I came out I didn't drink for ten years and I gave up cigarettes.

Curiously enough I sorted everything out in those three months. I decided that I'd come back to being a writer. Because I couldn't do anything I lay there and really, 'The Power of One' was written on the hospital ceiling over that three months. I plotted the whole thing out in my head.

Now my cholesterol is below normal, my blood pressure is below normal, but I have arthritis and take Celebrex for that.

People in my generation never looked after their skin. I go to the dermatologist once a year and get skin cancers blasted off, but they're the things caused in childhood. Now after a shower every night I put sorbolene on. I also put sun block on and wear a cap. But it's a bit late; I wish I'd known all those things 20 to 30 years ago.

When you're skating on thin ice, you might as well be tap dancing!

When you're skating on thin ice, you might as well be tap dancing. In other words, when you're out there you've got to give it everything you've got. That's been my total philosophy right through life. Take on more than you can chew and then chew like buggery!

Energy has never been a problem. We have a circle of friends, where energy doesn't come into it. You just do what you have to do, and that's more than most people anyway. I've always been somebody who's had energy, lots of energy. I seldom sleep more than four or five hours a night so I've got to fill those hours.

I just assume that you have energy. You just have it. I only know that I've got energy and I always wonder why people don't. I think energy is very much motivation. You watch people who are de-motivated, that need 12 hours sleep, they shush around, they don't do things and they put off things till tomorrow. It is a mental thing. If you're de-motivated or you're not motivated, you seem to lose the power to do things.

I have never actually been able to put into one day what I actually had planned for the day. It's always failing in the energy business. Even if I cut back my sleep to three hours, as I sometimes do when I'm writing a novel. I love the early mornings because that's where all the power is.

I'm not a spiritual person in the sense that I pray to any given God or religion, but I'm a deeply spiritual person in terms of environment and the process of being. Spiritual is a difficult word again. I'd like to think of myself as a moral person, a spiritually moral person. I don't like unfairness, greed, racism, and all the things that human beings do to other human beings appal me. I don't lie. I don't cheat. I wouldn't take advantage of anybody for my own benefit.

I answered the spiritual question to my son when he was dying. My son Damon was a haemophiliac and he got a blood transfusion that had the aids virus and he died over a long period of time. About three months before he died he said to me one night in hospital, 'Dad, am I going to go to heaven?' Even though he hadn't been brought up with concepts like that, it's a question that a kid asks when they know they're going to die. I said, 'Well, I don't believe there is a thing called heaven, but I will explain it differently. When you die, what your brothers and I are going to do is get a bag of cement, and a bucket of water, some sand and a trowel. And then after everybody's been to the funeral we'll heap aside the flowers and were going to build a little tombstone ourselves out of the cement and the bricks. It will be real crook you understand because none of us can do these things very well. When the cement is till wet, because you've spent your life so well, we're going to write the word WOW! on the cement and that's going to be your tombstone.

But where you're going to go from there. The worms are going to get you mate, and they're going to turn you into the most beautiful soil you ever saw. And we're going to plant a tree next to that little piece of cement with WOW on it, and its roots are going to go down and it's going to be nourished. It will grow beautiful green leaves and the leaves will give up oxygen. The oxygen will go into the air and the air will form clouds. The clouds will weep for you and they'll fill the lakes and the lakes will make the world all new again. Life will begin and you'll be a part of everything.'

The major thing in life is relationships
I love going out, my circle of friends is as good as any man could possibly wish to have. I have wonderful friends, whom I trust implicitly. Once a friend asks there's no refusal and that's a code that we have amongst us. You can't say no, so you make sure you ask reasonable things of your friends and that's a very good tenet for friendship. Don't expect the impossible from your friends.

I say the major thing in life is relationships, which includes your friends. It astonishes me when people say you're lucky if you've got a friend. I've got 50 friends I know I could absolutely depend on in any sort of crisis. Nobody would walk away from me, neither would I walk away from them.

I don't need to be motivated. I guess I'm reasonably wealthy, so that motivation doesn't exist. I write books and when the voices start in my head I can't ignore them. Motivation to write doesn't need to exist. I don't think this is a tedious business, writing a book. 12 hours a day for 7 months of the year never worries me. That's a product of my mind so I don't need to be motivated for that. I certainly don't need to be motivated for seeing new things or doing new things.

Motivation is such a weird word, it's such an overly used word today. You've got motivational experts as though there is a need to wind somebody up and point them in the right direction. I am astonished.

The blue planet is such astonishing miracle. You are actually given 70, 80 or 90 years of days like this. Of joyous friends, of lovemaking, of beautiful women, of ideas, of mental stimulation, of visual stimulation and you say people need motivation? It just seems crazy!

For me, it's one of the great enigmas. I don't understand why people need motivation to do anything, when the very process of life is such an astonishing miracle.

Chapter 14

The Secrets of Energy and Vitality Revealed

With such a variety of personalities and lifestyles – was there anything these inspirational people had in common? At closer examination, the answers are there.

A five and a half year study of 7,000 subjects in California (Belloc and Breslow 1965) showed that the most important feature of those who survived into a healthy old age was not their income, physical condition or genetic inheritance, but some simple lifestyle habits.

1. Sleep 7-8 hrs
2. Breakfast every day
3. Not eating between meals
4. Normal Weight
5. Regular Exercise
6. Moderate drinking (not more than 2 glasses alcohol per day)
7. Non-smoker

All the people interviewed for this book demonstrated these seven habits (with the exclusion of Bryce Courtenay, who didn't sleep as much). The Californian study also showed that life-span was proportionate to the number of the above habits that people had adopted. How many habits do you follow?

In addition Dr Stephen Jewett did a study in 1973 on 79 healthy people aged 87 years and older, which identified self-sufficiency as an important component of longevity. These following common elements were also identified:

1. Normal weight
2. Good muscle tone
3. Still drive a car
4. Engage in physical activity
5. Diet included a variety of foods, high in protein, low in fat

6. Early risers with 6-8 hours sleep
7. Moderate or no alcohol
8. Most drank coffee
9. Very little medication used (compared to general population)
10. A broad spiritual base
11. Followed career of their choice
12. Retired later in life
13. Not prone to worry
14. Keen interest in current affairs
15. Optimistic with a sense of humour
16. Viewed life as a great adventure
17. Not preoccupied with death
18. Adaptable, didn't dwell on the past, preferred to live in the present

These factors indeed fit the profile of those in this book, but let's take a closer look at the similarities in lifestyle of all the personalities interviewed.

Diet

Although some were very conscious about what they ate and others not so (or left it to their wives!), all ate what is considered a low fat, healthy diet. Sure, they had fish and chips or pizza occasionally, but it was not the norm. Their diets were balanced with fruit and vegetables, meat, chicken or fish, all grilled. The majority ate fish on a regular basis. They all had either wholegrain or rye breads and butter or marg, if any was sparing.

Sweets, desserts, chocolate, cakes, muffins etc, hardly figured except for an occasional treat, reinforcing the current feeling that these 'high glycemic' foods are not that good for you, or your waistline. Only one ate between meals!

The younger ones were more inclined to protect their health by taking supplements, whereas the older ones were not.

The majority realised the importance of their water intake, most drinking at least a litre per day, water in the car, water by the bed. When it came to alcohol, all of them drank wine or beer in moderation (except one on medication) and some an occasional whisky.

Exercise

They all were very aware of the importance of exercise and regularly did some form of exercise (walking, golf, aqua fitness, cycling, even running) 30 to 60 minutes on most days.

Health

It was surprising that some had had no major health problems, Karl being a good example. Most had, however, been through very challenging health problems, cancer, high blood pressure, high cholesterol, heart problems, stroke, hip replacements etc. What is notable is:

a) They all took action to correct any lifestyle habits, which might have contributed.

b) They are proactive in having regular medical check-ups, especially in the areas where they have a genetic pre-disposition.

c) All had surgery, took medication or did whatever was necessary to improve their condition as soon as it was diagnosed, instead of burying their heads in the sand as a lot of people do.

Body weight

As Ron Tacchi said, 'There are old people and overweight people – you never see old people who are overweight.' Most of the interviewees were slim and trim, well within healthy weight range guidelines. Two of them had weight problems from time to time, but were making an effort to keep them under control.

Non-smoker

As Dr John Tickell says, 'You can't be intelligent and smoke at the same time'. The evidence is loud and clear. None of those interviewed were smokers. Sure Karl, Bryce and Ron used to be heavy smokers, but they all gave up, and they never looked back. Life is too precious. They now enjoy life a lot more and they wouldn't dream of taking the risk of destroying their lives.

Mental health

All stressed the importance of looking after your mental facilities as well as your physical health, 'If you don't use it, you lose it.' Activities could be reading, learning about technology, learning a new language, finding a challenge at work. Studies on old rats showed that the brain actually responds to stimulation and the neurons grow more dendrites. Dendrites enable brain cells to communicate with each other. A long term study at Duke University also showed that there is no decline in intelligence as we get older, except in those with high blood pressure.

Skin care

Almost all the Australians interviewed in this book had experienced skin cancers and commented that the knowledge of sun damage was unknown in their youth. Most had had skin cancers removed and were now taking good care of their skin, staying out of the hot summer sun, using sun block, wearing a cap and generally covering up.

Stress relief

All had a constructive way for handling stress, in addition to admitting that they did not allow themselves to get as stressed as they once did when they were younger.
Exercise:
All used exercise as a means to relieve stress.
Relaxation Technique:
Most used meditation, visualisation, or meditative techniques such as focussing on a simple task like the dishes or lying on the floor and drifting off. More than 600 studies on transcendental meditation have shown that meditation lowers heartbeat, blood pressure and adrenaline levels.

Being serious

None took themselves seriously – my favourite saying is 'Life is too short to be serious'. They realised that most things in life are just 'small stuff', especially to those who have had major health scares.

With age we can gain maturity and get a bit of a laid back attitude. One of the best things about being older is that you do as you wish and don't feel you have to conform. You can say what is on your mind, dress as you like and feel comfortable. It does not matter if your car is old, as long as it gets you around.

Knowledge and wisdom

Most interviewees expressed sadness or concern that younger people didn't listen to the wisdom of those older. They felt they had a lot of information gained over the decades, which would help younger people. They had made mistakes, they had learnt the hard way, and the wisdom gained could save so many younger people from hardships and make the road, as Roger Climpson says, 'less bumpy'.

Getting out of bed

They were all early risers, some very early and liked to be up and at it, actively doing something, none of this of lying around moping. 'There's too much to do'. They grasped life with both hands.

Putting back

All were involved in giving back to the community through speaking engagements, giving time to charities, bushfire brigade and spiritual organisations. And all gave of their time to help with this book in the hope that it might help others.

No regrets

All realised that there is no point in having regrets because it just makes you miserable. A quote from the front of Toni

Lamond's autobiography by Elisabeth Kubler-Ross, says it all:
'Live so that you don't look back and regret that you've wasted your life.
Live so you don't regret the things you have done or wish that you had acted differently.
Live life honestly and fully.
Live.'

Life expectancy
No one wanted to linger on, or be a burden to their families, they wanted to go out with a 'bang', doing what they loved to do. Their vision of the future was continuing to do the things they do now, with less time 'working'. Regardless of age they expected to live another 10 to 20 years longer than their current age. Those who had already surpassed their own parents were extremely grateful for every extra day. As Toni put it so well 'aware that the days dwindle to a precious few'.

Always have a project
All had something to do, at all times, something they were interested in, something that challenged them. A hobby, an interest... a passion.

Keeping up to date
Maintaining their mental functioning was vitally important. Everyone kept up with the news and what was happening in the world, on a daily basis. All except two embraced technology, emails, faxes, mobiles, teaching themselves how to use a computer in their later years.

Belief in something
Whether they were Christian, religious or not, they all believed in something larger, some universal intelligence which was there to assist them in times of need. As Nancy and Toni both said there were many times in their careers when miracles happened, when 'someone/something'

had lent a helping hand.

Values

Being older means that you have a greater understanding of what is really important in life. What we felt was important when we were young and competitive is often no longer so important. All placed the utmost value on their health, realising that being able to maintain their quality of life was dependent on good health. Keeping in contact with friends and family was also extremely important. None placed value on material belongings or career success.

Attitude

All had a very positive and optimistic approach to life. They were honest in admitting that, like everyone, negative thoughts went through their minds and sometimes it was hard to get motivated. Using self-talk they were able to tell the mental voices to go away, to ignore them and press on.

Many had been through extremely tough times, the depression, poverty, and having to leave school at 14 or 15 to work. Their ability to survive these challenges made them stronger. Little things didn't stress them any longer, and they were extremely grateful for all the good things they had in their lives.

Everyone was very humble and expressed gratitude for having good health, great friends and family, and being able to maintain their lifestyle. They were proud to be called Australians and loved living in Australia.

The greatest secret of all for vitality and longevity

The one greatest thing that that every one of them said, loud and clear was:

Follow your passion, Follow your heart, Do what you want to do,

Do what you love to do, regardless of what age you are.

It is never too late!!!

Again I ask you, what images of ageing do you hold in your head? Are you following your passion, doing what you love to do? There is no time like now to focus on the positive aspects of ageing and take action, just like the people whose stories you've read and thousands of others like these:

Hildegard Ferrera, the world's oldest skydiver, who parachuted over Hawaii on her 99th birthday.

Otto Comanos, who took up windsurfing at 73 and was still surfing two to three times a week in Sydney, Australia, at the age of 89.

Kamato Hongo in Japan who at the age of 114 still sings and does 'teodori' a kind of slow posture dancing from her armchair.

James Talbot Guyer who at 74 base-jumped off the 148 metre high Perrine Bridge in Idaho, USA.

Kiro Gligorov, elected President of the former Yugoslav Republic of Macedonia at the age of 74 and still in office at 85.

Jeanne-Louise Calment, who lived until the age of 122 in France. She took up fencing at 85, was still riding a bicycle at 100 and portrayed herself at the age of 114 in the film 'Vincent and Me', the oldest actress in film.

Jenny Wood-Allen from Scotland, who ran her first marathon at the age of 71 and completed the London Marathon aged 90 years and 145 days.

Haywood Leroy Stewart, Colorado, USA, who was still performing as a lifeguard at 86.

John Glenn Jnr, USA, who at 77 became the oldest astronaut launched into space aboard Discover STS-95 in 1998.

Jack MacKenzie, Canada, who joined a ski expedition and reached the North Pole at the age of almost 78.

George Blain, Florida, USA, was still snowboarding at Steamboat Springs at the age of 86.

Adeline Ablitt, who at 95 'looped-the-loop' while a passenger in an unpowered glider in Leicestershire, England.

So what's your excuse?

Will you be joining me at my 100th birthday party?

References

Your Health is in Danger   Robert G Allen
    Churchill Trust 1998

Stop Ageing Now!   Jean Carper
    Harper Collins 1997

Ageless Body, Timeless Mind   Deepak Chopra
    Ebury Press 1993

The New Nutrition   Dr Michael Colgan
    Apple Publishing 1996

Younger at Last   Steven Lamm MD
    Pocket Books 1998

Real Age   Michael F Roizen MD
    Harper Collins 1999

Balance Your Body, Balance Your Life Edward A Taub MD
    Kensington Publishing 2000

Ageing Well   George Vaillant
    Scribe Publications 2002

START FEELING YOUNGER RIGHT NOW!!

GENTLE EXERCISE VIDEOS

Slender Secrets Volumes 1 & 2

These highly motivational videos featuring a variety of age groups and sizes are targeted at those wanting to lose weight, but are SUITABLE FOR ANY LOVER OF GENTLE EXERCISE.

A 35 minute home exercise program to suit everyone's fitness level. Routines can be done at three levels – Regular, Half Pace or seated in a chair.

Keep The Bounce In Your Step

Motivational home video features seniors, but is suitable for anyone wanting a light exercise program.

A 30 minute exercise session to suit everyone's fitness level and includes floor exercises and stretching. Routines can be done at three levels – Regular, Half Pace or seated in a chair.

FIVE MINUTE FITNESS BOOK

"The perfect book for every couch potato who thinks fitness means pumping iron and running marathons. Carol shows just how easy it is to put a little exercise into your life – and keep it there. Sensible, practical and fun." – Diane Parks, Editor, Slimming Australia

Easy ideas for keeping in shape while watching TV, talking on the phone or working at the office. Includes instructions for using the Dyna-Band Total Body Toner.

DYNA-BAND TOTAL BODY TONER

A rubberized exercise band which exercises all major muscle groups- upper and lower body! Five Minute Fitness Pack includes book and Dyna-Band.

Pink - Older Adult   Green - Women
Purple - Men   Silver - Athlete

Fitness Company International
Website: www.feelyounger.com.au
Email: info@feelyounger.com.au
PO Box 304 Matraville NSW 2036
Australia
Ph (612) 9311-3235